Black Recreation

A Historical Perspective

Jearold Winston Holland

University of Wisconsin—La Crosse

Burnham Inc., Publishers

Chicago

President: Kathleen Kusta
Vice-President: Brett J. Hallongren
General Manager: Richard O. Meade
Project Editor: Sheila Whalen
Design/Production: Tamra Campbell-Phelps
Cover: "Fishing Partners" by Bernard King
Printer:

Library of Congress Cataloging-in-Publication Data

Holland, Jearold W.
    Black recreation : a historical perspective : playing through turmoil
/ Jearold W. Holland.
        p. cm.
Includes bibliographical references (p.   ) and index.
    ISBN 0-8304-1576-9 (pbk.)
    1. Recreation--Social aspects--United States--History. 2. African
Americans--Recreation--Social aspects--History. I. Title: Playing
through turmoil. II. Title.
    GV14.45 .H65 2002
    306.4'8'08996073--dc21

                                                                2001006941

Manufactured in the United States of America

The paper used in this book meets the mini-
mum requirements of American National
Standard for Information Sciences—
Permanence of Paper for Printed Library
Materials, ANSI Z39.48-1984.

For Theresa,
Bradley,
Mackenzie, and
Lukas,
my wife and children

CONTENTS

ACKNOWLEDGMENTS

Few books can be written without the assistance and support of competent assistants. I owe a great deal of gratitude and special thanks to the following individuals: Leslie DeVries was my graduate assistant throughout a significant portion of the writing of the manuscript. Leslie is without a doubt one of the finest graduate students I have had the opportunity to work with. She spent many hours gathering data, discussing the content of the book, providing editorial comments, and being a good student and friend during the development of the manuscript. Sandy Sieber, program assistant in the Department of Recreation Management and Therapeutic Recreation at the University of Wisconsin at LaCrosse provided technical assistance in producing much of the text. Sheila Whalen provided valuable insight while editing the manuscript. Professor Anita Barta, recently retired, has been my unheralded mentor. She has been my sounding board and has lifted me up when I needed to be lifted and brought me back on course when I have strayed. Ira Hutchinson and many members of the Ethnic Minority Society of the National Recreation and

Park Association have provided insightful information that added significantly to the manuscript. Theresa, my wife of more than twenty years and my best friend, was the final editor of the book. She and I have ventured through similar projects in the past. Without her continued encouragement and support, the manuscript would not have come to completion.

INTRODUCTION

The idea for this book grew for several distinct reasons. First, as an African-American educator of recreation and leisure, I have a professional and personal interest in the play, recreation, and leisure of all Americans including blacks. It is my contention that much can be learned about people through investigations of how they engage or have engaged in recreation. Investigations of this type are fascinating as these phenomena have a definite impact on quality of life. Essentially, life would be hard to endure without some significant degree of play, recreation, or leisure. Second, due to numerous conversations with recreation students, practitioners, and educators regarding a lack of material historically documenting blacks and their experiences in recreation and leisure in the United States, the issue calls for attention. Educators like myself have an obligation to advance perceptual and indisputable deficiencies in their professional fields.

To this point, any significant chronological or longitudinal account of the black experience in recreation does not exist or, at best, is vague and fragmented. Those interested in play, recreation,

and leisure—including educators, practitioners, and students—
find it difficult to locate historical accounts of blacks and their
experiences in recreation. Aside from the more generally respected
accomplishments that blacks have made in the well-publicized
sports-recreation arena, much of the information on blacks in
other broad recreation activity has been infrequently, at best only
sporadically, documented.

Nevertheless, chronological and historical descriptions of the
recreation profession, of many of its professionals, and of women
have been documented. Several leisure-studies scholars have provided comprehensive historical descriptions and analyses of significant events of recreation and leisure in the United States[1] and
other countries. These analyses have addressed the play, recreation,
and leisure of early primitive societies of Egypt, Greece, and Israel,
continuing through Europe's, Dark and Middle Ages to the
Renaissance, and have discussed the free-time activities of different
cultural groups, including Americans, up to the development of
modern parks and recreation.[2]

Foster Rhea Dulles, in his book *A History of Recreation: America
Learns to Play*,[3] wrote one of the first and most highly regarded historical descriptions of recreation. Dulles provided one of the most
extensive accounts of the history of play and recreation in America
from the 1600s through the early 1960s. Dulles's analysis provides
evidence that the recreation of early Americans was influenced by
several societal traditions, and the most obvious and important
was probably the puritan work ethic. This ethic was necessary in a
world subject to extremely harsh living conditions coupled with
intrinsic belief in the moral value of work.The earliest settlers had
to focus on work in order to survive. These values were powerful
because it was a basic fact of life that if the settlers did not devote
practically all of their time and energy to their work, they could not
endure the harsh realities of their new settlement. Not until
around the eighteenth century did the colonists begin any significant quest for and expansion of a broad range of recreation and
play pursuits. This quest was the result of demographic changes
which added significantly to the urbanization of America.

Dulles's chronological depiction is exceptional and detailed.
However, there is little mention of blacks in this dissection. For
example, the incorporation of slavery into American life allowed
significant contributions to the play, recreation, and leisure of

whites and blacks, yet Dulles failed to adequately discuss or explain this significant contribution. In retrospect, it would appear that blacks, based on many early chronological accounts, had very little impact on recreation and leisure in America or elsewhere. In reality blacks as individuals brought to a developing nation (against their will), had a definitive impact on the recreation of white Americans.

The initiation of slavery as an American institution gave whites more time to amuse themselves with the many pleasures of the period including hunting, fishing, attending cock fights, socializing, and drinking. Dulles's evaluation is clearly rendered from a majority point of view because, although he provides a rather explicit account of whites and their recreation in early America, little mention is made of the play, recreation, and leisure of blacks. Dulles fails to address or explain the importance, type, or impact of recreation in the slave's, or black person's, cultural life.

In most cases when blacks are mentioned in the historical recreation and leisure literature, scholars acknowledge the extremely harsh discrimination they suffered. Yet seldom do they provide specific examples and implications of such discrimination. In other rare instances, blacks are mentioned in light of their assumed limited contribution to the recreation and amusement of whites, especially during the slavery period, supporting the notion that they had no recreation of their own. This brings to light an implicit assumption that blacks did not engage in their own recreation and certainly did not grasp the elusive concept of leisure. Along with this assumption comes the notion that whatever recreation skills blacks displayed were ones they developed when they were brought to America.

It was after slavery that noticeable changes in the play, recreation, and leisure status of blacks occurred. After slavery, whites began to pay more (although extremely limited) attention to blacks and to see recreation from broader points of view. However, because of the superior position whites held in American society, their attention to blacks was often critical. Many labeled and stereotyped blacks as unsophisticated and lacking certain play, recreation, or leisure skills and interests. This judgment was fundamentally unfair because newly freed blacks were just learning to recreate in a dominantly white and prejudiced America. Logically, when any person learns anything new, including a new game or activity, mistakes and misinterpretations can and should be expected and an incremental learning process anticipated. More important, human beings have always learned more by participating than by watching, and in early America, blacks (slaves) were "officially" allowed only to watch whites recreate and engage in leisure. In essence, any lack of play, recreation, and leisure proficiency was to be expected, especially when it was evaluated by the majority race in a prejudiced society.

Only more recently has the impact of race and culture been addressed in the historical analysis of play, recreation, and leisure; and even these attempts have been sporadic. For example, it is not as uncommon today to find issues concerning minority, ethnic, cultural, and racial groups and their recreational interests and involvement addressed at professional meetings, including recreation and leisure conferences. As one example, abstracts from the 1999 Leisure Research Symposium at the National Recreation and Park Association provide some verification of these attempts.[4] More recreation professions are adopting agendas that address race and recreation in America. However, in most instances when these issues are addressed, they provide little information about the history of non-white groups in recreation in America, nor do they attempt to explain how the current play, recreation, and leisure attitudes of these groups may have been affected by their history.

These sporadic attempts are interesting in light of the fact that most demographic forecasters, even those in the recreation field, predict a vastly different population constituency for the United States and the recreation profession as we continue into this millennium.[5] America is at present an ethnically, racially, and culturally diverse society, as nonwhites comprise the majority population of all major cities,[6] and our population will become even more diverse in the future. It is estimated that minority group members will constitute more than 25 percent of the workforce early in this millennium. It is further estimated that North America will have a significantly different ethnic minority group makeup, in that all minority groups combined will comprise more than 50 percent of the total population.[7] The projected sociodemographic profile of the nation is a driving force behind the attention given to racial diversity in America. The impetus pushing more racial and ethnic diversity relates to expected significant increases in of racial minority groups.

Some in the recreation and leisure profession believe that the extent to which the makeup of population will change is greatly exaggerated and that the impact of ethnic change will be felt in only a limited number of U.S. states.[8] Implicit in this reasoning is that unless one lives in a major metropolitan area, these statistics are not a great concern. This thinking may have detrimental over-all effects on leisure-service educators and practitioners. Many may pursue professional paradigms without significant discussion of race, diversity, and culture. In a human service enterprise, one whose business has a great deal to do with people's satisfaction, students must be educated in a way that will make them productive practitioners and knowledgeable universal citizens.

The data is not entirely conclusive, but it may be true that only larger U.S. cities will initially feel the reality of changing demographics. A more visionary perspective does not support this assumption, and not all professionals are so pessimistic. Two recreation and leisure scholars, Bob Riley and Thomas Skalko, countered this pessimism when they wrote in an article in *Parks and Recreation*, "Although ethnic diversity may be more fully realized in specific regions of the country, the profession must be poised to address the multicultural nature of the global environment."[9]

Regardless of the broadness of the demographic change, this alteration in the make-up of America will require an understanding, sensitive, and ethnically in-tune recreation and leisure profession. The profession will have to find ways to succeed in its service delivery in the light of future demographics. Also, recreation professionals will need additional accurate and thorough information on the various cultural constituents they serve in order to operate efficiently in a racially diverse society. In this respect, there is a need for additional information on the cultural experience, particularly the black experience, including its play, recreation, and leisure.

In response to such service demands, the profession has begun to pay more attention to this deficiency. More and more recreation professionals are receiving information that can make them more efficient when interacting in such a diverse society. Professional recreation and leisure conferences are inviting speakers with research agendas focused on the minority recreation experience. The National Recreation and Park Association (NRPA), the leading professional association, has taken a lead in this area. For example, at the 1999 NRPA conference in Nashville, Tennessee, a number of presentations and selected poster sessions were aligned with underrepresented groups and the recreation experience.[10] Yet to date there has been no successful attempt to address the longitudinal black recreation experience.

While the black experience in America has been told in many ways, it has seldom, if ever, been substantially addressed from the play, recreation, and leisure perspective. That is the primary intent of this book. In part, the book aims to support a more diverse curriculum initiative. Practically every higher education institution has made some attempt to demonstrate more diversity in its curriculum. A current trend in higher education includes acceptance of more cultural or minority studies, particularly African-American studies. Many universities have begun to apportion substantial resources in the effort to expand minority-enhanced curriculum agendas and programs. Paradoxically, this growth of interest in academic higher education has not paralleled the same interest in other areas of academe such as affirmative action, hiring policies, and race-based scholarships. Instead, these initiatives have been under constant scrutiny, as many perceive them to be forms of reverse discrimination. At the same time many visionary administrators in colleges and universities are encouraging faculty to include more diverse perspectives in their teaching.

One might ask, Why is the recreation and leisure paradigm a useful means of exploring the black experience? Addressing this question requires that we look from the quality-of-life perspective. To a significant degree, the recreation and leisure profession has built itself on this perspective. It might be said that one measure of personal quality of life is (among other factors including happiness, wealth, and health) what is done in individual and group recreation or leisure. One can gain significant understanding of the black experience through historical analysis of black involvement and participation in play, recreation, and leisure in America. Historical interpretation, accurately presented, can help give individuals a better sense of identity, of who they are and how far they have come.[11] All will benefit, majority and minority, by being provided with broad-based perspectives regarding all individuals—including whites, blacks, and other minority groups—and by investigating the opportunities available in terms of play, recreation, and leisure.

Due to past neglect and discriminatory attitudes, blacks have largely been excluded from the literature on the history of recreation and leisure. For a recreation professional, it is troubling to consider the number of texts written on the early history of recreation and leisure that contain only limited mention of blacks, almost as if blacks did not exist in the United States or elsewhere. Again, inherent in this assumption is the implication that blacks had no influence on the development of play and recreation in America. Only recently has scholarly inquiry begun to openly address some of the broad dimensions of the race and recreation and leisure topic. This book helps to fill a fraction of that void.

As society appears to be more or less in transition, when the terms *blacks* and *African Americans* are still used interchangeably, I will follow this style. In this book the major focal points will encompass presenting, describing, and explaining historical data and its influence on African-American recreation and leisure. This process may create better understanding of black play, recreation, and leisure. The process will show that blacks, contrary to some myths, have never had a chaotic culture; that play, recreation, and leisure were important and significant in the black experience; and that blacks contributed significantly to white recreation and leisure.

The book is divided into major sections. The prologue briefly addresses conceptual boundaries of race, culture, play, recreation, and leisure in America, putting these terms into general perspective. Importantly, none of these terms carries a universally accepted definition, even among those more intimate with recreation and leisure studies. This lack of consensus makes empirical application of the terms to a given context somewhat problematic. Therefore, I have defined them in a context appropriate, I feel, for understanding black recreation and leisure. After this, a current recreation and leisure framework for blacks in America is provided. This includes a broad analytical description and discussion of where America stands regarding black involvement in recreation and leisure. The reader may find the writing in this section somewhat more research-oriented or academic in tone. The remaining sections, the bulk and heart of the manuscript, provide historical information that accounts for the current situation of the play, recreation, and leisure of blacks in America. More specifically, part 1 will provide a descriptive analysis of blacks and their recreation prior to and including the slavery period in the United States. Part 2 will provide an account of the development of recreation and leisure from slavery's end, through the separate-but-equal period, up to the famous 1964 *Brown v. Board of Education* decision which dismantled the separate-but-equal law of the land. The preceding periods in history represent distinctive shifts in America's racial attitudes and behaviors, and each had a significant impact on black culture, including its recreation and leisure. Part 3 briefly provides conclusions and summary information. Throughout the book, preceding selected major sections, short hypothetical stories are intended to help guide the reader to a better understanding of ensuing material.

Notes/References

1. See the following for more comprehensive historical accounts of recreation: Foster S. Dulles. 1965. *A History of Recreation: America Learns to Play*, 2nd ed. New York: Meredith Publishing Company; Benjamin K. Hunnicutt. 1988. *Work Without End: Abandoning Short Hours for the Right to Work.* Philadelphia: Temple University Press; John P. Robinson, Geoffrey Godbey, and Anne J. Jacobson. 1997. *Time for Life: The Surprising Ways Americans Use Their Time.* University Park, PA: Pennsylvania State University Press.

2. Richard Kraus. 1997. *Recreation and Leisure in Modern Society,* 5th ed. Menlo Park, CA: Addison Wesley Longman, 159–84.

3. Dulles.

4. Abstracts, Paper, and Poster Presentations. 1999. Leisure Research Symposium, National Recreation and Park Association Congress, Nashville, TN, October 20–24. Published by the Department of Leisure Studies—University of Illinois; Department of Recreation and Leisure Studies—University of Georgia; and the NRPA.

5. Christopher Edginton, Debra Jordan, Donald DeGraaf, and Debra Edginton. 1995. *Leisure and Life Satisfaction: Foundational Perspectives.* Madison, WI: Brown & Benchmark, 344; Robinson and Godbey, 220–25; B. Riley and T. Skalko. 1998. The evolution of therapeutic recreation. *Parks and Recreation* Parks and Recreation 33, no. 5 (May): 65–71.

6. L. Younghill and K. Thomas. 1996. Multicultural sensitivity: An innovative mindset in therapeutic recreation practice. *Parks and Recreation* 31, no. 5 (May): 50–52.

7. Ann M. Morrison. 1992. *The New Leaders: Guidelines on Leadership.* San Francisco: Jossey-Bass, xii.

8. Geoffrey Godbey. 1997. *Leisure and Leisure Services in the 21st Century.* State College, PA: Venture Publishing, 106.

9. Riley and Skalko, 67.

10. Abstracts, Paper, and Poster Presentations.

11. D. White. 1999. *Ar'N't I a Woman: Female Slaves in the Plantation South.* New York: W.W. Norton, 3.

Prologue

RACE, CULTURE, EQUALITY, AND RECREATION IN AMERICA

Before one can address race as an issue for African Americans, there must be some fundamental discussion of race and racial equality. Early American forefathers attempted to clarify equality succinctly in the Constitution when they declared that "All men are created equal." Although these words were clearly written, they did not appear to pertain to blacks.[1]

When Africans were first brought to America and throughout their enslavement, race was the most salient factor in determining their quality of life. During slavery blacks were subjected to some of the most horrendous conditions a human being could endure. They were molested, beaten, starved, humiliated, degraded, and mutilated. Many did not survive their enslavement since they could be tortured and even killed for major and minor offenses. Yet, as a people they survived. Most of the negative treatment was brought on because of their race. Obviously then, race was the most significant determinant of quality of life in early America.

Since blacks were brought to America as slaves, some progress has been made. Slavery no longer exists. Laws have been passed which outlaw discriminatory behavior and practices. Yet, even with this incremental progress, many blacks continue to believe that their race remains a major determinant influencing their quality of life.[2]

There has been increased scholarly interest in the issue of whether or not race still significantly determines quality of life for blacks in America. An essential question is: Is race declining in significance relative to other quality-of-life determinants such as intelligence and social class?[3] A more appropriate question in the context of this book is: Does intelligence, class, or race significantly determine participation in recreation and leisure activity and quality of life for blacks? There is no clear-cut answer, and scholars have reached very different conclusions regarding the impact of race in America.

There are continued claims of progress in racial equality in America. With all the presumed progress, however, some scholars continue to challenge the notion of racial equality. One of the more notable attacks on racial equality was *The Bell Curve: Intelligence and Class Structure in American Life*, written in 1994 by the late Richard J. Herrnstein, a professor of psychology from Harvard, and Charles Murray, a research fellow at the American Enterprise Institute. In *The Bell Curve*, Murray and Herrnstein reached the conclusion that America is divided into socioeconomic as well as "cognitive classes" of individuals. In their overall analysis they asserted the racial superiority of whites over blacks. Murray and Herrnstein used a number of IQ studies as the base for their analysis, and concluded that blacks have an average IQ of about 85 as compared to about 100 for whites. Further, they postulated that IQ is determined more by genetics than by environment (as most other scholars contend). In essence, according to Murray and Herrnstein, blacks are genetically intellectually inferior to whites.[4]

Another prominent scholar, Arthur Schlesinger, in his acclaimed book *The Disuniting of America: Reflections on a Multicultural Society*, took a different approach in accounting for racial differences, as he addressed multiculturalism in America.[5] Schlesinger's argument was that the world has always mixed its people and that too much attention to the racial and cultural differences of Americans will have negative consequences for the country as a whole. In Schlesinger's view, "The point of America was not to preserve old cultures, but to forge a new *American* culture."

Finally, William Julius Wilson, a black scholar in Harvard University's Afro-American studies department, in his book *The Declining Significance of Race: Blacks and Changing American Institutions*, made the argument that race has become less important than class as a determinant of life chances for blacks.[6] Wilson concluded that the black underclass experiences limited mobility and access primarily due to lower-class status, while there has been an upsurge in mobility for middle- and upper-class blacks, due mainly to their class position. Murray and Herrstein's, Schlesinger's, and Wilson's arguments suggest the extent of dissension over the status of race as a determinant of quality of life in America.

Race and Culture in America

Andrew Hacker, in the book *Two Nations: Black and White, Separate, Hostile, Unequal*, wrote,

> Every one of us could write a book about race. The text is already imprinted in our minds and evokes our moral character. Dividing people into races started as convenient categories. However, those divisions have taken lives of their own, dominating our culture and consciousness, coloring passions and opinions, contorting the facts and fantasies.[7]

Hacker appropriately captures the impact that the race phenomenon has had on most Americans. Although continually on the minds of many, the concept of race and all that comes with it is elaborate.

The issues of race and culture, because they still represent complex and sensitive domains, present a significant challenge for society and for the recreation and leisure profession. It is important to understand that many of society's most delicate concepts—like race, class, gender, culture and other identity variables—do not exist independently.[8] In most instances they overlap and interact with one another to such a degree that complete separation is virtually impossible.

To be sure African Americans, like all persons, are as individual as persons can be. Even in their play, recreation, and leisure, blacks display a degree of diversity that makes it virtually impossible to imply that there is any such thing as *"black recreation or leisure."* Some blacks and non-blacks even question whether there is anything that can be described as *"black culture."* Randall Kennedy, a black professor in Harvard University's law school, wrote in the May 1997 issue of *The Atlantic Monthly*, that the notion that *".* . . Black people should have a special, closer, more affectionate relationship with fellow Blacks than with others" is not accurate.[9] Dr. Kennedy rejects the concepts of racial unity and ethnicity as important to blacks or to any racial or ethnic group.

However, many of society's most eloquent intellectuals and writers document race as a constant and, indeed, important variable impacting today's society.[10] Cornell West and Dinesh D'Sousa are two prominent writers on race in America. Although they agree that race is an issue, they have different views regarding its pervasiveness. D'Sousa advances the idea that racism is real but can be overcome. He maintains that most of our essential assumptions about racism are wrong and that society should omit individual racial classifications. West, on the other hand, contends that race matters in much of the nation's current affairs and that for most blacks (and whites) race is often the most important factor in their successes and failures. Both viewpoints are loaded with positives and negatives, and there does not appear to be a clear, correct answer.

It is not always wise for professionals and laypersons to focus so much on the terminology. One can get lost in the terminology and lose sight of the bigger issue. Currently, the focal point should be the importance of the *perception of race* for the individual. If race is thought to be an important determinant for an individual, it must be given serious attention in dealing with that individual.

Various terms are currently used in the race and culture arena. An in-depth analysis of each term is beyond the intent and scope of this book, but a rudimentary discussion may be necessary. The many commonly used terms include: culture, race, ethnicity, assimilation, acculturation, and diversity. There are numerous resources which professionals may consult to gain better understanding of the terminology. For example, well-known leisure scholars such as John Dattilo and Kathleen Shelton attempted a descriptive analysis of the terms for therapeutic recreation professionals in their article "Multiculturalism in Therapeutic Recreation: Terminology Clarification and Practical Suggestions."[11] In this endeavor, writers and scholars in recreation are making some significant attempts to help clarify racial and multicultural terms through articles and professional presentations.[12]

Culture has been technically defined in many ways. The concept is so difficult to define that definitions have been put into categories including descriptive, historical, normative, psychological, structural, and genetic.[13] One definition states, " Culture can be defined as an organized body of behavior patterns which is transmitted by social inheritance, that is, by tradition, and which is characteristic of a given area or group of people."[14] This definition contains the general characteristics of many other common definitions. That is, culture is seen as a human product transmitted through society by way of teaching and living. As such, for most intellectuals culture is a learned system of meaning and behavior that is passed from one generation to the next.

Culture is a difficult concept to completely understand. Some have postulated that race and culture are very closely connected. While this may be true in many instances, it is not always the case. It is not the color of a person's skin that makes him or her identify more with others having the same skin color or that determines whether these persons share a similar culture. Rather, cultural heritage is usually shaped by the shared experiences of individuals, including influences on their social and political environments. In a sense, black culture is made from a unique perspective on local and national ideals.

Race is also difficult to define. One definition describes race as "an arbitrary classification system of populations conceived in Europe, using actual or assumed genetic traits to classify populations of the world into a hierarchical order, with Europeans superior to all others."[15] To further compound the issue, even the construct of "race" is suspect[16] because there has been so much mixing of different races that modern physical anthropologists are not easily satisfied that individual races can be so easily separated from one another. Nevertheless, especially since slavery, America has been fixated on race. Consider the "one drop" rule. The "one drop" rule was developed by whites as a method of determining who was white—or privileged—and who was not. Using this construct, if a person had one drop of any blood other than white in his or her system, he or she was considered non-white.

Today, with the current status of race mixing in America, it is virtually impossible for anyone to escape the likelihood of having more than one blood ancestry. The U.S. Census Bureau is under scrutiny because of the racial identity categories used on its reporting forms. For the most part, the census asks Americans to identify themselves as white, black, or other. As the population in America becomes more biracial and multiracial, many individuals, proud of their heritage, want more accurate race categorization. Many of these persons advocate for more racial categories on the census forms, including specific biracial and multiracial categories.

Nevertheless the census bureau and some racial groups have been reluctant to include such categories. The census bureau's main objection is that including more racial categories complicates data tabulation. Other racial groups, especially some with smaller total numbers, also oppose additional racial categories for fear that their total numbers would be even more diminished. Jeffery Passel, the Urban Institute Immigration Policy Director,[17] provided information which helps to explain the complexity of the classification issue. Passel estimated that approximately 126 possible biracial or multiracial categories could be listed on census forms, creating an administrative nightmare for the census bureau. Still, one has to question the rationale of the census bureau. Is concern for administration and management more important than the gathering of potentially more accurate racial identification?

The race issue is not a problem everywhere in the world. In fact, during the 1920s Mexico stopped gathering race information for its census reports. However, race plays a more significant role in America because of an individual's personal perceptions or the perceptions of others. Racial identity is a very personal issue for Americans. For some individuals race means everything—it engulfs their sense of being. For others race means very little—they view themselves in a context of individualism. Some people don't want to talk about the politics of race, while others seem infatuated with the issue. With all of its variety, race appears to be what society or an individual makes of it.

The race issue spreads far and wide. Some observers claim that certain minority group members "play the race card" when faced with potential injustices. Two prominent figures have been accused of playing the race card in high-profile cases. From the Clarence Thomas Supreme Court confirmation, in which Thomas stated that Anita Hill's accusations were nothing but the "high-tech lynching of a black man," to the famous O.J. Simpson murder trial when the media suggested that race may have been a factor in Simpson's arrest and indictment, race has been brought into the limelight.

Regardless of whose views are most correct, Americans seem fixated on race. It is difficult to read a newspaper or listen to a major news program without race relations being mentioned. Yet, there are few significant interactions between blacks and whites in the United States in which race is not a factor. The importance of race invades virtually all aspects of life, from music to sports. Some of today's musicians consistently refer to race in their songs. Rap singers speak of black professional athletes with white wives and of white policemen mistreating black men. Some successful musicians such as Darius Rucker, the black lead singer from the group Hootie and the Blowfish, and prominent actors such as Denzel Washington and Danny Glover call attention to discriminatory attitudes and behaviors that they and others continue to encounter. Professional black athletes articulate discriminatory practices in player positions and coaching. Black schoolchildren continue to complain about discriminatory practices in their schools. Elderly blacks are reluctant to enter many long-term care facilities for fear of discriminatory attitudes and behaviors of white employees. After more than 100 years since slavery's end, race continues to be laden with emotion.

One of the most successful young golfers in the world has had the issue of race raised by the media. Tiger Woods is multiracial, the product of a particular ethnic mix. Tiger's mother is half Thai, one-quarter Chinese, and one-quarter Caucasian; his father is half African, one-quarter Chinese, and one-quarter Native American. Nonetheless, the offspring of this marriage is identified in America as a black child. When Tiger was very young, his father identified him, as do many black parents of biracial children, as African-American. Later in life Tiger rejected this lineage and termed himself "Cablinasian."[18] To some this may seem insignificant. Why not just use the traditional classification to categorize Tiger? Don't make it a big deal. This is not an issue for everyone, but for some it is. Many older blacks have indicated to me their disappointment with Tiger's self-identification. Relying on the ways that whites have traditionally identified who is black, coupled with the fact that Tiger obviously has some black lineage and is arguably the best golfer in the world, some older blacks feel Tiger is not proud of his black lineage. But only Tiger can say if this is significant to him.

Race is seldom a neutral element; indeed, it produces power-ful emotional responses. The race issue spreads far and wide and reaches the poor and wealthy, the educated and uneducated. In an era of political correctness, it has become difficult to speak about race without fear of retribution—being labeled a racist, one with-out racial sensitivity, or one who plays the race card for advantage. These labels are applied to the least educated as well as the most educated. For example, in Texas minority lawmakers demanded the resignation of a University of Texas law professor who said that black and Mexican-American students cannot compete academi-cally with white students, in part because their cultures do not encourage achievement.[19]

Many African Americans' feelings about race are summed up in the words of Richard Wright in his highly acclaimed book *Black Boy*. Wright wrote:

> At last we were at the railroad station with our bags, waiting for the train that would take us to Arkansas; and for the first time there were two lines of people at the ticket window, a "white" line and a "black" line. During my visit at Granny's, a sense of two races had been born in me that would never die until I died.[20]

In the minds of many Americans, both black and white, the lines between the races seem to have grown so blurred that it is dif-ficult to distinguish them from one another. On the surface, blacks seem to be faring much better with regard to gaining equality with whites. Some current research and facts seem to confirm this. For example, compared to earlier periods, blacks now earn more money than in the past, and some have gained access and oppor-tunity in areas previously closed to them, including education, housing, sports, industry, politics, etc.

Yet, for many other African Americans, the lines are still clear; and many contend that the races are growing further apart. A body of research also confirms these beliefs. For example, in one of the more recent analyses of race in America, Theodore Rueter's book

The Politics of Race: African-Americans and the Political System[21] reports the following:

- The infant mortality rate among blacks is more than twice that of whites.
- Almost one-fourth of all blacks between the ages of eighteen and twenty-nine are in prison, on probation, or on parole.
- Nearly half of all U.S. murder victims are black.
- Blacks account for about 30 percent of all AIDS cases, although they represent only 12 percent of the population.
- More than 40 percent of all black children live in poverty.
- Black children are three times more likely than whites to live in a single-parent household.

If that were not enough, another group of scholars added this information:

- Black unemployment has been consistently higher than white.
- The black poverty rate has been consistently worse than the white rate.
- Whites' wealth is more than four times that of blacks.[22]

These findings suggest major differences between blacks and whites in terms of opportunity.

With such a potentially emotional and divisive topic, the concept of race and all that it embraces demands attention from the recreation professional. As previously mentioned, professional recreation publications like the *Therapeutic Recreation Journal* and the *Journal of Leisure Research* have recently begun to invite scholars to address race and multiculturalism in the profession. Some scholars have accepted these invitations and have begun to provide unified definitions and practical suggestions for the recreation professional.

Yet a consensus definition of the vocabulary and understanding of race and multiculturalism has not been achieved. Without such consensus the recreation professional will find it difficult to adequately understand multicultural phenomena. Many terms are used interchangeably, which can add to the confusion. For example, "multiculturalism" and "diversity" have different meanings but are often used as synonyms. The same can be said of "culture," "ethnicity," and "race." A number of articles and texts have been written to foster an understanding of the terminology, but perhaps the most important aspects of multiculturalism deal with the degree to which an individual assimilates into the broader society. "Assimilation or acculturation is the process by which one enters, is comfortable, absorbs, learns, acquires, and integrates the overt and covert cultural characteristics of another culture."[23]

Play, Recreation, and Leisure

To many, the concepts play, recreation, and leisure are identical, but to recreation professionals, these terms technically are distinct. Theories and definitions of these constructs forwarded by prominent recreation scholars have been significantly dissected, divided, dismembered, combined, restructured, and reinterpreted throughout the years. A lack of consensus is likely to continue. Like resolving the issues in the race arena, coming to an in-depth understanding and common definition of play, recreation, and leisure is beyond the scope and intent of this book. Each is multidimensional and varies in complexity. As previously mentioned, this book does not intend to confound the general analysis due to nonconformity of professional terminology. Yet, a basic discussion of each concept will help to facilitate a more accurate, general, and preliminary understanding of the impact of state of mind, free time, social status, etc., on the play, recreation, and leisure of blacks throughout history.

Play

More than fifteen theories of play have been proposed over the past century, and none has been explained in a way to satisfy everyone. The numerous theories of play have included:

- The surplus-energy theory: Play is motivated by the need to burn up excess energy.
- The recreation theory: The purpose of play is to restore or

conserve energy when one is exhausted.
- The instinct-practice theory: Play enables youngsters to practice skills necessary for adult life.
- The catharsis theory: Play serves as a safety valve for the expression of bottled-up emotions.
- The recapitulation theory: Play is a way of passing information from generation to generation.
- The self-expression theory: Play is a method of self-expression.[24]

For the most part, play has been connected with the activities of children. For a child, play is work. It's what they do. Children do not take time off to play. Ask a child what he or she is going to do today, and they will most often reply "play." Many psychologists and play specialists believe that a child whose play is significantly interrupted may face serious psychological problems in life. Ruth Russell, an accomplished recreation scholar, defines play thus: "Play is a spontaneous act. It involves the carefree suspension of consequences, a temporary creation of its own world. Play is not for the sake of a final goal; it is motivated by the enjoyment of living."[25]

The point must be made that adults play too. Adults have always engaged in play and playfulness throughout history. Play in an adult's life is multidimensional. Adults play with their children and with other adults; they play children's games, cards, sports, and numerous other pursuits. However, adult play is generally thought to be less muscular and more intricate in detail, involving more rules and regulations, than children's play.

Recreation

Recreation, on the other hand, is not as challenging to define as play. Recreation has been widely viewed as an activity, engaged in during one's free time, which is pleasurable and has socially redeeming qualities.[26] Within the context of this definition is the assumption that recreation is a voluntary pursuit involving positive and socially acceptable behaviors. The Latin translation of the word recreation encompasses the two terms *to restore and to refresh*. Most dictionary definitions of the word include self-refreshment or self-restoration.[27] One of the most important subcomponents of recreation is that it is voluntary and does not occur because of compulsory or obligatory outside pressures.

Leisure

Leisure is probably the most elusive and the most difficult to define of the three terms. In the past forty years a number of factors have been used to help identify and define leisure experience.[28] There appear to be five salient factors most often agreed upon:

1. Leisure in the classical view, is a state of being in which activity is performed for its own sake.
2. Leisure is a social-class attribute.
3. Leisure is free or unobligated time.
4. Leisure activity is carried on in free time.
5. Leisure is a state of being indicated by perceived freedom.[29]

Leisure is most often thought to be freely chosen relative to the constraints of other human behavior.

Conceptually leisure has to do with happiness. For recreation professionals, their curricular training tends to present leisure as the most significant element of happiness. It is not. Other things more or less under our control are also essential to happiness. The first is a moral standard by which to guide our actions. The second is satisfactory home life in the form of good relationships with family and friends. The third is some form of work which justifies our existence and makes us good citizens. After these have been addressed, we can begin to think of leisure as an ingredient of happiness.[30]

Through a careful analysis of the concept of leisure, it is reasonable to assume that when blacks were enslaved in America they had little, if any, leisure. Their time, movements, and independence were strictly controlled. Even when not attending to the requirements of slave labor, slaves were required to be in certain places at specific times and engaging in specified activity. In order to work effectively during daylight hours, the slave had to get enough sleep to restore the body. In this respect, even non-work hours afforded slaves little if any leisure. The term "recreation" probably comes closest to describing black activity outside mandatory work obligations, during slavery. Recreational activities were engaged in by slaves in their free time, and they were pleasurable compared to the burdensome work routine. However, to the extent that recreation is defined as voluntary and not pursued due to outside pressures, how can it be accurately applied to the slave's life?

In this book the term *play* will be used primarily as it relates to the activities of children. Although *recreation* and *leisure* do not have the same meanings (though most laypersons do not distinguish between the two) they will be used more or less interchangeably here.

Understanding Black Leisure

To truly understand African Americans as a group is difficult, and it should be, as it should for any given group. Given similar data, writers and scholars have come to distinctly contrasting conclusions about the nature of blacks and their situation in America. While most of the information about the status of blacks in America has been in the areas of income, occupations, relations with whites, and levels of education, much less attention has been given to recreation and leisure differences between whites and blacks.

In a relatively recent book entitled *Time for Life: The Surprising Ways Americans Spend Their Time*, John Robinson and Geoffrey Godbey, two leisure scholars from the University of Maryland and Penn State University, deduced four types of time available to Americans: contracted time, committed time, personal time, and free time. Contracted time was defined as time spent working. Committed time covers family and household roles. Personal time includes such biological necessities as eating, sleeping, and grooming. Finally, free time includes the leftover activities that, in all probability, involve greatest individual choice.[31]

Robinson and Godbey used time diaries as their research method when describing how Americans spend their time. Time diaries are personalized accounts of an individual's daily life. Other than interviews, time diaries are one of the most valid methods for accurately detailing individual activity. Beginning at a specified time, often at midnight, time diaries ask individuals what they did, where they did it,who was with them, and whether they were doing anything else at the same time. Although they are potentially excellent research methods, time diaries have their limitations. The most significant are truthfulness of participants and completeness or accurateness of information provided. Many individuals are reluctant to provide a researcher with the most intimate details of daily life, and in addition they may not provide the most complete details needed for thorough data analysis. For example, a member of a metropolitan youth gang may be reluctant to provide detailed accounts of his or her activity because of relationships with other gang members or potential consequences of revealing possibly unlawful activity. Nevertheless, time diaries provide useful data about how Americans spend their time.

Since the enactment of the 1964 Civil Rights Act, many scholars have supported the notions of either convergence or divergence of blacks and whites in many areas of American life. Some believe that blacks and whites have converged, that the gaps between the races have narrowed in the areas of individual earnings, occupations, and education.[32] These scholars argue that Americans are more alike ideologically, educationally, and vocationally today than in the last thirty years. Yet, many other American scholars point to divergence, or more separation of the races.[33] This divergence perspective encompasses more dubious losses and gains, which complicates the picture. Robinson and Godbey's time diaries detail both convergence and divergence between blacks and whites.

Robinson and Godbey hypothesized, and subsequently found, that blacks showed *convergence* with whites in contracted time (paid work), committed time (household/family care), and personal time, and they found *divergence* in certain free-time activity. Though the findings were stimulating, the authors point out that they were based on a limited sample of black study participants. Overall, it has been observed that African Americans have two to three more hours of free time each week than whites.[34] These analyses call for further discussion. For example, the convergence in contracted time was attributed to societal adherence to affirmative action guidelines and to equal-employment-opportunity legislation. While many of the barriers to education and vocational opportunity have been reduced, others continue to prevent true equal opportunity for blacks. Informal networking in the employment arena is an example of a barrier that continues to limit black vocational opportunity, while reliance on standardized educational achievement tests unjustly puts many blacks at the lower end of the educational achievement scale.

Robinson and Godbey find convergence of blacks and whites in committed time, which includes housework, childcare, and shopping, and attribute this similarity to the shift of labor from manufacturing to an information/technology workforce. Further they found overall convergence in personal time that includes sleeping, eating, and grooming. Interestingly, these leisure scholars found blacks spent more time grooming than whites and attribute this to blacks' struggle to maintain a "proper image in the white-dominated business and social world"[35] and to the belief that looking good helps a person feel good, which, in turn, assists in coping with the pressures of racism in America. This is an interesting deduction, but Robinson and Godbey, maybe unconsciously, perpetrate a stereotypical American bias that may impact equal opportunity. Who can say empirically that looking good will help blacks cope with racism? If this is true, isn't it true for all individuals?

Robinson and Godbey also found divergence in free-time activity between whites and blacks. There appeared to be more differences in church attendance, television viewing, and listening to the radio or music, with blacks engaging in these activities significantly more than whites.

Theoretical Differences in Black and White Recreation Participation

From the 1950s to the 1980s America saw an increase in scholarship and writing about blacks in recreation. Richard Kraus, one of the most prolific scholars in the recreation and leisure field, observed during this period that more research examining the recreation patterns of various minority groups, including African Americans, had been completed.[36] Interestingly, the vast majority of the investigation which has been reported on the recreation and leisure experiences and participation patterns of blacks has been in the area of outdoor recreation[37] or has been focused on blacks in urban areas. Importantly, the majority of this research has found that blacks and whites differ in what they spend on various forms of entertainment, and in their involvement in outdoor recreation. Thematically, this scholarly inquiry indicates that blacks are more dispersed in such outdoor activities as camping and hiking, and tend to be more involved in social and urban-oriented activities like basketball, football, dancing, and attending church.

Much of the data continually indicates that blacks underutilize, or differently utilize, certain types of recreational and leisure programs and facilities, especially state and national parks, than whites.[38] Most of this analysis was conducted through national and statewide surveys which have also shown that African Americans are disproportionately underrepresented in recreation participation at state and national parks. Similar results have been obtained for urban park settings.

What accounts for this disproportionality? A number of recreation and leisure scholars have examined possible reasons for unbalanced participation between blacks and whites. Generally these inquiries have yielded interesting but often incompatible theories. Most writers have aimed their inquiries at one of two areas: a) investigating differences between racial groups (for example, looking at differences between blacks and whites), or b) investigating differences *within* racial groups (considering factors such as income, community, gender, and education). The reason for these differences in leisure interest and participation has been an issue of considerable debate in the leisure profession. Two theories accounting for these differences proliferate in the leisure literature: the *marginality theory* and the *ethnicity theory*.[39]

Marginality Theory

Randel Washburne was one of the first and probably the most articulate scholar to describe the effects of marginality and ethnicity in a leisure context. Washburne's interests were primarily in the outdoor recreation area. Using marginality and ethnicity, Washburne attempted to explain why blacks participated less than whites in outdoor recreation.

The marginality theory suggests that persons with homogenous socioeconomic status are more likely to participate in similar recreation activities. The theory supports the idea that differences in recreation participation and behavior are functions more of social status and class than of race. This theory rests on the assumption that differences in recreation and leisure participation patterns are influenced by the collectively lower socioeconomic position of blacks in America. In short, blacks as a group are considered on the "margins of society," and do not have the same opportunities as whites—or they do not perceive the white majority's recreation as their own.

The marginality theory attributes recreation participation differences to differences in opportunities afforded to individuals and groups. In recreation and leisure, these opportunities are often associated with the availability and accessibility of recreational facilities. This theory indicates intentional and unintentional discriminatory practices and attitudes in the recreation and leisure service industry, and advances the idea that provision of recreation and leisure opportunities has been most prevalent for the white majority and in white communities.

A substantial research base supports this paradigm while demonstrating that racial and ethnic discrimination may affect recreation and leisure choices.[40] Because of discriminatory practices, some blacks have opted for alternative recreational and leisure choices rather than subject themselves to prejudicial treatment in the recreation industry.

Some leisure professionals and laymen who contend that recreation is a voluntary enterprise reject the philosophical underpinnings of the marginality theory and have concentrated more on discrimination as a reason for participation differences. James Murphy, a prominent leisure scholar from San José State University, is one of these professionals. Murphy rejects the marginality notion and comments,

> Oppressed racial groups, including blacks, have never been able to engage in leisure pursuits as the advantaged Anglo citizen, whatever their social class or occupation, because of discriminatory practices, insufficient discretionary money, and inadequate leisure opportunities and services available in their community.[41]

In other words, regardless of their position in society blacks have not been welcome in recreation activity outside their immediate communities.

Other observers find that the geographic region in which a person lives may have an impact on recreation participation. For example, southern African Americans tend to participate in inexpensive, close-to-home forms of leisure.[42] This brings to the forefront the idea that residential location may have a significant impact on recreation and leisure interest and involvement.

Nevertheless, some evidence lends support to the marginality theory. These findings suggest that individuals from similar socioeconomic backgrounds, regardless of race, are more likely to engage in similar recreation and leisure activities. It is not uncommon to find, for example, that middle-class blacks participate in activities similar to whites. Activities of this type include traveling and metropolitan activities,[43] such as attending the symphony-concerts-theater, dining in restaurants, and attending professional conferences. Research also indicates similar leisure patterns for whites and blacks from lower social classes compared to those from the middle class.[44]

Ethnicity Theory

In contrast, the ethnicity theory supports the proposition that an individual's subculture determines differences in interest and participation. In this instance, ethnicity refers to the cultural characteristics of an individual, for instance Native American, Italian-American, Mexican-American, African-American, etc. Inherently, this theory calls for an acknowledgment of differences in leisure involvement between ethnic and racial groups. A person's culture may account for rather unique societal barriers or opportunities, and may foster a tendency towards participation in certain activities and a reluctance to participate in others. In other words, blacks do not have high participation numbers in such activities as golf, ice hockey, tennis, and skiing because they are likely to be considered by many blacks as "white" activities. Some blacks, according to this hypothesis, believe these activities are designed by whites and have the interests of whites at their core. This theory calls for acknowledging differing expectations, values, and norms based on racial and ethnic identification.

Some leisure research supports the proposition that recreational involvement is significantly influenced by culture, race, and ethnicity.[45] For example, blacks have low participation rates in such outdoor activities as hiking and camping, but have higher participation rates in social and urban-oriented activities such as picnicking.[46] In this respect, recreation and leisure can be tools for differentiating between cultural, racial, and/or ethnic groups.[47] In yet another study comparing black and white leisure interests, Steven Philipp, a prominent recreation scholar, compared individuals with similar socioeconomic characteristics and found significant differences in the ratings of appeal and comfort they gave to certain activities. Philipp concluded that discriminatory practices in many areas of American life—housing, employment, and education—extend to recreation and park settings. He commented that much of the prevailing behavior and interest of blacks is attributed to historic patterns of discrimination and to feeling unwelcome in varying leisure interests.

Golf could fit Philipp's assertion. Well into the 1990s many golf courses did not welcome or even allow blacks as members. Tiger Woods is racially mixed, as noted earlier, and one of today's most famous golfers, but he mentions in some of his 1997 television commercials that he does not feel comfortable playing some courses because of his racial heritage.

One particular recreation and leisure study in 1990 considered the effects of social class and race in eleven leisure activities and found that participation was based more on race than on social class.[48] Steven Philipp, in one of his more recent studies, examined the appeal of recreational activities among middle-class whites and blacks and found notable differences between the races in more than half of the activities identified. These investigations provide empirical support for the ethnicity proposition. Regardless of social class, individuals in a given racial or ethnic group may vary in leisure preferences compared to members of other racial and ethnic groups.

Drawing concrete conclusions about recreation interest and involvement due to the ethnicity theory is not conclusive. Many variables confound the analysis. For example, one set of leisure scholars observed significant leisure association between blacks and whites who perceived themselves to be middle-class, and no association between those blacks and whites who perceived themselves to be poor or working-class.[49] These same writers found significant association between the recreation and leisure preference of blacks from different social class categories. Further, in a different study, the same group of researchers expanded their analysis and discovered that black females who identified themselves as poor and working-class were more closely correlated with similarly positioned black males and with females who identified themselves as middle-class. Their recreation preferences were different from those of poor working-class whites and from middle-class black men.[50] What this analysis revealed are some potentially strong relationships between both black and white females and males at the middle-class level, but no strong relationship between groups at the poor or working-class level.

What does this mean? It is likely that different racial and ethnic groups, and individuals from within these groups, will experience different leisure constraints and attitudes. Again, a number of studies have documented specific differences in recreation participation among racial and ethnic groups; however, research directed towards understanding these differences is limited. Addressing subjective and empirical reasons for variance is a logical progression.

Opposition to Marginality and Ethnicity Theories

Although leisure educators have advocated the marginality and ethnicity theories for many years, critics argue that they do not explain all cultural and racial participation differences. Myron Floyd of Texas A&M University has been one such critic. Floyd is one of the most widely published scholars on race and recreation. In his essay *Getting Beyond Marginality and Ethnicity: The Challenge for Race and Ethnic Studies in Leisure Studies Research*, he attempts to explain why marginality and ethnicity are ineffective in describing racial participation differences. Floyd advances the notion that both concepts are ambiguous and have not been adequately defined. He further implies that both marginality and ethnicity are based on erroneous hypothetical assumptions. For example, according to the marginality theory "the reduction of socioeconomic barriers should lead racial and ethnic minorities to exhibit leisure preferences valued by the dominant group." At the same time, the ethnicity theory "suggests that assimilation in its latter stages weakens ethnic ties and produces behavioral styles similar or identical to mainstream society."[51] Floyd makes the point that both ideological assumptions specify *how to address leisure differences* and not the *actual causes of the differences*.

Floyd goes even further in his evaluation of racial and ethnic research in leisure and examines the limitations of methodological approaches including: measurement of race and ethnicity; controlling for socioeconomic differences; and small sample sizes. Floyd is accurate in his discussion of limitations in methodological approaches; however, ethnic and race researchers of recreation and leisure need not reinvent the wheel. A substantial amount of research in the social sciences, minority studies, psychology, and education fields help clarify and explain the definitional concepts which Floyd has difficulty standardizing.

A third theory has been offered to account for differences in racial participation patterns. It is identified by another well-respected leisure scholar, Steven Philipp, as "racial discrimination."[52] This theory, while not as widely discussed or accepted in the recreation field, is based on discrimination and prejudice due to skin color. It is potentially the most personally and professionally divisive of the theories. It is personal because it requires practitioners within the recreation profession to acknowledge racial discrimination in the profession. This theory applies the notion of intentional and institutional racial discrimination to understand and explain participation differences. The theory cuts across both the marginality and ethnicity theories, and is rooted in some of society's most blatant racial realities. It provides an explanation that may account for how a well-educated and successful black individual can receive negative differential treatment in many areas of recreation.

All three theories have some degree of support and research to bolster their basic assumptions. However, large gaps remain in the literature that tries to account for the variations in recreation and leisure behavior of blacks. For example, William Julius Wilson, the noted race researcher from Harvard University, proposed the class polarization perspective which has been used to explain differences between the most oppressed blacks and those who are middle-class. In this viewpoint blacks have been able to take advantage of more opportunities.[53] This perspective maintains that as blacks gain better access and opportunity, they will engage in pursuits similar to those of other races in the same social class.

Wilson's class polarization perspective is not shared by all. Many blacks, even many who have managed to negotiate society's racial waters relatively successfully, insist that race is still a significant issue in their lives. Many successful blacks contend that the advancements made have been relatively limited. They continue to argue that overt, covert, and institutional racism remain more significant than social class in limiting their advancements in society.[54]

Which, if any, of these theories, ideas, or philosophies realistically accounts for the current play, recreation, and leisure status of African Americans? A presentation and analysis of blacks and their experiences in these areas prior to slavery, during slavery, and after slavery will assist us in drawing a conclusion.

Notes/References

1. Charles Johnson and Patricia Smith. 1998. *Africans in America: America's Journey Through Slavery.* New York: Harcourt Brace & Company; Derrick A. Bell. 1987. *And We Are Not Saved: The Elusive Quest for Racial Justice.* New York: Basic Books, 23–50.

2. Cornel West. 1994. *Race Matters.* New York: Vintage Books, 17–31.

3. M. Thomas and M. Hughes. 1986. The continuing significance of race: A study of race, class, and quality of life in America, 1972–1985. *American Sociological Review* 51: 830–41.

4. Charles Murray and Richard Herrnstein. 1994. *The Bell Curve: Intelligence and Class Structure in American Life.* New York: Free Press.

5. Arthur Schlesinger. 1992. *The Disuniting of America: Reflections on a Multicultural Society.* New York: W.W. Norton & Co., 13.

6. William Julius Wilson. 1980. *The Declining Significance of Race: Blacks and Changing American Institutions,* 2nd ed. Chicago: University of Chicago Press, 145–54.

7. Andrew Hacker. 1992. *Two Nations: Black and White, Separate, Hostile, Unequal.* New York: Macmillan Publishing Company, ix.

8. Deborah White. 1999. *Ar'N't I a Woman: Female Slaves in the Plantation South.* New York: W.W. Norton, 4.

9. Randall Kennedy. 1997. My race problem—and ours. *Atlantic Monthly* 279, no. 5 (May): 55–66.

10. Dinesh D'Sousa. 1995. *The End of Racism: Principles for a Multicultural Society.* New York: Free Press, ix.; West, 17–31; David K. Shipler. 1997. *A Country of Strangers: Blacks and Whites in America.* New York: Knopf, 4.

11. John Dattilo and Kathleen Shelton. 1997. Multiculturalism in therapeutic recreation: Terminology, clarification, and practical suggestions. *Therapeutic Recreation Journal* 31 (3): 148–59.

12. The following is a list of professional presentations by the author on blacks in recreation:

- National Park and Recreation Association. 1999. Blacks in recreation and leisure. Poster presentation, Nashville, TN, October.
- Research Association of Minority Professors (RAMP). 1999. The recreation of blacks in America. Paper presentation, Washington, DC, February.
- National Park and Recreation Association. 1999. Blacks in recreation from slavery to present. Poster presentation, Nashville, TN, October.
- American Alliance for Health, Physical Education, Recreation and Dance. 1996. Minority issues in therapeutic recreation. Atlanta, GA, March.
- Midwest Symposium on Therapeutic Recreation. 1996. Leisure motivation of African-American adolescents. Paper presentation, St. Louis, MO, May.
- Midwest Symposium on Therapeutic Recreation. 1995. Developing Community Programs in Therapeutic Recreation. Paper presentation with copresenter Mary Lechnir, Springfield, IL, May.
- Midwest Symposium on Therapeutic Recreation. 1994. Assessing the Minority Client in Therapeutic Recreation. Paper presentation, Milwaukee, WI, April.
- Midwest Symposium on Therapeutic Recreation. 1993. African American Faculty and Practitioners in Therapeutic Recreation: Problems and Implications. Paper presentation, St. Louis, MO, April.

The following abstracts, papers, and poster presentations were delivered at the 1999 Leisure Research Symposium, National Recreation and Park Association Congress, Nashville, TN, October 20–24. Published by the Department of Leisure Studies—University of Illinois; Department of Recreation and Leisure Studies—University of Georgia; and the NRPA.

- K. Henderson (University of North Carolina—Chapel Hill). Researching Leisure and Physical Activity with Women of Color: Issues, Answers, and Emerging Questions.
- J. Mak (Indiana University). Gender and Ethnicity Issues of Doctoral Students in the Field of Recreation, Park, Tourism, and Leisure Studies
- K. Shinew (University of Illinois at Urbana-Champaign) and M. Floyd, (Texas A & M University) The Association of Interracial Contact and Leisure Preferences
- T. Tedrick and R. Boyd (Temple University). Older African-American Men and Leisure
- K. Henderson (University of North Carolina—Chapel Hill) and B. Ainsworth (University of South Carolina). Enablers and Constraints to Walking for American Indian Women: The Cross Cultural Activity Participation Study.

13. A. L. Kroecher and C. Kluckhohn. 1952. Culture: A critical review of concepts and definitions. Harvard University, Cambridge, MA, Papers of the Peabody Museum of America Archaeology and Ethnology, vii.

14. Ibid., 48.

15. C. Christensen (1989). Cross-cultural awareness development: A conceptual model. *Counselor Education and Supervision* 28: 270–87.

16. Shippler, x.

17. Jeffery Passel. 1998. Urban Institute Immigration Policy Director. Multiracial issues and the 2000 Census. C-SPAN TV show/conference, June 5.

18. Jack Clary. 1997. *Tiger Woods.* New York: Smithmark Publishers, 9–10.

19. *Chronicle of Higher Education.* 1997. September 15.

20. Richard Wright. 1944. *Black Boy.* New York: Harper Brothers, 46.

21. Theodore Rueter. 1995. *The Politics of Race: African-Americans and the Political System.* New York: M.E. Sharpe, Inc., 5–24.

22. Lucius J. Barker, Mack H. Jones, and Katherine Tate. 1999. *African-Americans and the American Political System,* 4th ed. Upper Saddle River, NJ: Prentice Hall, 32–53.

23. Dattilo and Shelton, 148–59.

24. Richard Kraus. 1997. *Recreation and Leisure in Modern Society,* 5th ed. Menlo Park, CA: Addison Wesley Longman, 24–55.

25. Ruth Russell. 1996. *Pastimes: The Context of Contemporary Leisure.* Madison, WI, and Dubuque, IA: Brown & Benchmark Publishers, 50.

26. Richard Kraus. 1990. *Recreation and Leisure in Modern Society,* 4th ed. Glenview, IL: Scott, Foresman/Little Brown, 42–47.

27. Christopher Edginton, Debra Jordan, Donald Graaf, and Debra Edginton. 1995. *Leisure and Life Satisfaction: Foundational Perspectives.* Madison, WI, and Dubuque, IA: Brown and Benchmark, 40.

28. Ibid., 32–48.

29. Kraus (1990), 48–54.

30. G. Fallodon. 1920. Address delivered at the Harvard Union, 8 December 1919. Published by the Riverside Press/Houghton Mifflin (Cambridge, MA), 3–5.

31. John Robinson, Geoffrey Godbey, and Anne J. Jacobson. 1997. *Time for Life: The Surprising Ways Americans Spend Their Time.* University Park, PA: Pennsylvania State University Press, 11–13.

32. Reynolds Farley, James A. Davis, and John Modell. 1984. *Blacks and Whites: Narrowing the Gap?* Cambridge, MA: Harvard University Press, 6–15; Richard Freeman. 1976. *The Black Elite: The New Market for Highly Educated Black American.* New York: McGraw Hill, 1–40.; R. B. Hill. 1981. *Economic Policies and Black Progress: Myths and Realities.* Washington, DC: National Urban League Research Department, 39–46.

33. Hill, ibid.; H. Bryce. 1973. Letters from readers: On the nature of black progress. *Commentary* 56 (August): 4–19; Alphonso Pinkney. 1984. *The Myth of Black Progress.* Cambridge, MA: Cambridge University Press, 1–17.

34. Robinson and Godbey, *Time for Life,* 222.

35. Ibid., 221.

36. Kraus, 1997, 127–30.

37. M. Floyd and J. Gramann. 1993. Effects of acculturation and structural assimilation in resource based recreation: The case of Mexican Americans. *Journal of Leisure Research* 25: 6–21.

38. Randel Washburne. 1978. Black under-participation in wildland recreation: Alternative explanations. *Leisure Sciences* 1 (2): 175–89.

39. D. Carr and D. Williams. 1993. Understanding the role of ethnicity in outdoor recreation experiences. *Journal of Leisure Research.* 25 (1): 22–44; Ira Hutchinson. 1987. Ethnicity and urban recreation: Whites, blacks, and hispanics in Chicago's public parks." *Journal of Leisure Research* 19: 205–222; Washburne, Black under-participation.

40. Randel Washburne. 1978. Report 20, Outdoor Recreation Resources Review Commission Study. Washington, DC: U.S. Government Printing Office; Washburne, Black under-participation.

41. James Murphy. 1974. *Concepts of Leisure: Philosophical Implications*. Englewood Cliffs, NJ: Prentice-Hall, 95.

42. S. M. Stamps and M. B. Stamps. 1985. Race, class, and leisure activities of urban residents. *Journal of Leisure Research* 17 (1): 40–56.

43. M. D. Woodard. 1988. Class, regionality, and leisure among urban black Americans: The post civil rights era. *Journal of Leisure Research* 20: 87–105.

44. Stamps and Stamps, 40–55.

45. Kraus, 1997, 127–30.

46. J. Dwyer and P. Godster. 1992. Recreation opportunity and cultural diversity. *Parks and Recreation* (September): 22–31.

47. Russell, 329.

48. J. Dwyer and R. Hutchinson. 1990. Outdoor recreation participation and preferences by black and white Chicago households. In J. Vinning, ed., *Social Science and Natural Resource Management*. Boulder, CO: Westview Press, 49–67.

49. Myron M. Floyd, K. Shinew, F. McGuire, and F. Noe. 1994. Race, class and leisure activity patterns: Marginality and ethnicity revisited. *Journal of Leisure Research* 26 (2): 159.

50. _____. 1995. Gender, race, and subjective social class and their association with leisure preferences. *Leisure Sciences* 17: 75–89.

51. Myron Floyd. 1998. Getting beyond marginality and ethnicity: The challenge for race and ethnic studies in leisure studies research. *Journal of Leisure Research* 30 (1): 3–22.

52. Steven Philipp. 1995. Race and leisure constraints. *Leisure Sciences* 17: 109–120.

53. William Julius Wilson. 1978. *The Declining Significance of Race*. Chicago: University of Chicago Press; William Julius Wilson. 1980. *The Declining Significance of Race: Blacks and Changing American Institutions*, 2nd ed. Chicago: University of Chicago Press; William Julius Wilson. 1987. *The Truly Disadvantaged: The Inner City, the Underclass, and Public Policy*. Chicago: University of Chicago Press.

54. C. Marrett. 1980. The precarious position of the black middle class. *Contemporary Sociology* 9: 16–19; Thomas and Hughes.

Part One

Chapter One

BEFORE SLAVERY

We turn our attention now to issues surrounding the life and treatment of early American immigrants, Africans, and slaves. In particular, some of the more salient portions of the cultural heritage of Africans, including their recreation and leisure prior to slavery are highlighted, such as the most prevalent African play, recreation, and leisure survivals in America.

Playing Free No More

For most communities in colonial Africa, life was a challenge encompassing all the traditional obstacles to survival. In most cases those obstacles included predatory animals; oppressive heat; sickness; and the struggle to maintain adequate nourishment, find clothing, and prepare shelters. Even so, life was generally rather predictable. For the most part, the people were happy and content. Africans were good workers and spent much of their time attending to the basic necessities. Colonial Africans, however, also took time

to enjoy life by engaging in meaningful social and community relationships through playing games, making music, singing, and dancing. They were especially proficient at singing and dancing, and
they took a certain amount of joy and pride in their competence in
these activities. Sometimes in their free time Africans congregated to
play music on their instruments and dance. It was a beautiful sight
to behold. They danced fast; they danced slow; but most of all they
danced with feeling, they danced with spirit. They danced for the
pure enjoyment it brought them.

*It was a typical warm day in the West African country we know
as Liberia. African men, women and children went about their
usual tasks. Men were farming, hunting, tending to livestock,
resting, socializing, and building shelters; women were also
farming, cleaning, washing, and preparing food for their families. Children were playing with one another in the open spaces
surrounding their parents' dwellings.*

*Baba and his wife Goa lived on the outskirts of the local
village of Damut (located about five miles inland from the West
African coast) with their four children: Simi, age 18; Nerod,
age 17; Tehe, age 15; and Ali, age 12. This was an especially
happy day because Baba and his family were preparing for the
wedding that evening of their daughter Simi to one of the village's young men. While Goa, Simi, and Ali were busy getting
ready for the joyous occasion by gathering fruits and vegetables,
cleaning, and decorating, Baba, Nerod, and Tehe were on a
hunting trip to find meat for the wedding dinner.*

*Baba was proud that he had helped rear two strong,
healthy boys, and now it was time to show them the fine art of
completing a successful hunt. Hunting, especially killing a
young man's first boar, was a rite of passage into African man-
hood. Hunting skills would be essential if the boys were to succeed in taking care of their future families, and it was also an
activity that African fathers yearned to share with their sons.*

*Apart from conflicts with other African tribes, the hunters
feared only the wild animals they might encounter on a hunting trip away from the close surroundings of Damut. Nerod and
Tehe were excited. This would be their first significant trip away
from home and into unfamiliar territory. The boys still had
much youthful playfulness in their blood, and they liked to brag
and boast to anyone willing to listen.*

Baba, Nerod, and Tehe were surprised when they saw the white men—as many as fifteen of them—standing before them. They were the first white people the African hunters had ever seen. In a country full of black Africans, anyone so different, so inconceivable as a white person seemed outside the realm of possibility. Yet there they were. Although the Africans were curious, they were not afraid. The white men seemed friendly.

Eventually, the men conversed, then dined and drank together, and the white men introduced the blacks to a new drink with a very potent alcohol content. That night, as the men ate and drank together, the black men began to feel the effects of the "spirits" and began to dance, eager to display their skill. The white men marveled at their performance, so the blacks danced and drank while the white men drank and watched.

The effects of the alcohol on the blacks was far more pronounced than on the white men, who were used to the drink. Eventually, the Africans became very intoxicated, losing their rational decision-making abilities. They were utterly vulnerable.

The next thing that Baba, Nerod, and Tehe recalled was waking up shackled with other unfamiliar African men and women on board a large ship. The white men whom they had befriended were now prowling the ship with guns and whips, ordering the captured blacks to do as they were told. The white men treated their captives as less than human. They beat them, made fun of them, starved them, raped them, tortured them. And they murdered them. For the first time in their lives Baba, Nerod, and Tehe were not free; they had lost their freedom and life would never be the same again.

They had lost their freedom while engaging in one of the activities they liked best: dancing. Baba, Nerod, and Tehe would never come back to Goa and Simi. Their lives would be forever changed. The family was separated. The women would forever ask where their men had gone.

Immigrants and Blacks in America:
The Early Years

Once settled, America began to grow at an alarming rate as numerous individuals—some free, some indentured, and some slaves—came to the country from around the world. One would think that, as a newly emerging democratic country, America would be eager to show gracious hospitality to its newest arrivals. But not all of those new arrivals were treated equally. White immigrants, indentured servants, and African slaves—all new to the country—received very different treatment. White immigrants were received best and were generally welcome, though some had to contend with religious or ethnic biases. Indentured servants could gain independence after periods of servitude if their masters were honest. African slaves received the most dreadful reception and treatment possible. They were viewed as less than human and were expected to serve white owners for their entire lives.

As time went on Americans grew concerned about the large numbers of individuals migrating from foreign lands. How could America accommodate the various needs and wishes of its new arrivals and still establish a culture of its own? Sometime during the 1800s America's social engineers were satisfied that relatively equitable assimilation of immigrants arriving from Europe and other foreign lands could be achieved.[1] However, such assimilation was difficult and in many ways unrealistic, because a system or model that could accommodate such diverse peoples had not been adequately developed, structured, or planned. America was the first to give it a try.

It was also unrealistic to believe that any immigrant could be totally assimilated without continuing some native traditions. It is very difficult to totally disengage oneself from all traditional cultural foundations. So America's social engineers compromised and determined that assimilation was successful if the sociocultural attitudes and practices of selected immigrant groups were not in conflict with the sociocultural structure and practices of the dominant American society. There were problems with this thinking: For example, who would be charged with determining the appropriateness or conflict of another group's sociocultural structure and attitudes? Was there some established formula for making this decision?

Ira Hutchinson, a well-respected black scholar in leisure studies, described this situation:

> As the compromise of theory and reality began to manifest itself in actual practice, the various immigrant groups were faced with

a major problem; namely how could they best fulfill their own social and cultural obligations without simultaneously being deprived of vitally needed social and economic services. On the one hand, they deemed it fitting and proper for their members to adopt and practice the attitudes, customs, and habits of the dominant society that would enhance their chances for socio/economic survival or improvement. On the other hand, immigrant ethnic groups decided that it was their primary responsibility, with or without the support of the public sector, to perpetuate and protect the sanctity and practices of those indigenous customs and traditions important to the group. In turn, the public sector accepted an increased responsibility for serving the basic socioeconomic needs of the destitute immigrant minority groups that chose to affiliate with the cultural organization of their adopted home.[2]

Hutchinson's analysis suggests the public sector's obligation to address the cultural interest of America's newest arrivals. Being a young and developing nation, America took pride in its hospitality and welcomed white immigrants with open arms. Indeed as a new nation, America sought to expand its population. The most efficient way to grow and prosper was to accommodate new arrivals.

In regard to the cultural needs of Africans who were brought to America as slaves, the white public sector made no such accommodations. This was primarily due to the way whites, as a group, viewed blacks: whites viewed blacks as inferior. This view was based on preconceived stereotypical biases. Blacks were less than human, so they did not deserve to preserve their cultural roots.[3] This attitude for the most part determined white tone and behavior toward blacks throughout their early years in America. To better understand these new American arrivals, it is important to analyze certain aspects of early African life.

Preslavery African Heritage

Americans are encouraged and taught from birth to be visionary and to focus on the future. As a result we tend to forget the lessons of the past. Indeed, the past is sometimes viewed as something that *ought* to be forgotten. However, if used analytically the past can provide significant insight into our present condition as well as our future. Importantly and historically, all groups—African Americans and other ethnic and racial groups—have turned to their native lands for better understanding of their identity as Americans. The influence of American blacks, and consequently their recreation and leisure, is rooted in the period before slavery, so we must briefly revisit Africa and some of its customs.

Africa is a continent rich in topographical beauty and diversity. There are numerous rivers, lakes, mountains, and grasslands within its borders. The peoples of Africa learned to adapt and develop proficiency in various skills in order to survive, so Africans from different regions could be very different in many of their customs and cultural beliefs, yet similar in others. Early Africans did what people everywhere did in order to survive and enjoy life: they hunted, they fished, they held family and community gatherings and celebrations, they sang, they danced, and they played with one another. Life in Africa was bound by traditions, and most early African empires had a hierarchical form of governance,[4] which generally meant that a king ruled and his subjects followed.

When slave ships arrived on African shores, many Africans were captured and their lives took a turn for the worse. The transition from a free life in Africa to life in bondage in America had a significant impact on blacks' play, recreation, and leisure habits. Some maintain that it was the institution of slavery that most affected blacks and their play, recreation, and leisure patterns, but this affirmation may overshadow other very significant contributors.

In fact, the institution of slavery itself may not have had the most significant impact. It may have been the particular *style* of slavery in America that produced the greatest impact on African Americans and their play, recreation, and leisure.

While it is true that slavery was also a part of African life, the situation in America was far less humane. Some Africans were familiar with the overall concept of slavery prior to their arrival in America, but American slavery had farther-reaching and longer-lasting psychological effects on Africans.

Certainly, slavery anywhere, even in Africa, was unpleasant. Yet in Africa most slaves retained many basic human rights and retained some hope of eventual emancipation.[5] In Africa slaves could be central members of community life, so, despite their distress, many Africans brought to America probably clung to some hope that slavery in America would be no different from—

and might be better than—slavery in Africa. At least initially, there may have been some optimism. Perhaps they could work themselves free from their burdens or obligations. Obviously, for those blacks who had never been slaves in Africa, slavery in America was devastating.

Many of those captured and awaiting transport to America could not bear the thought of servitude in a strange land. They entertained, and followed through with, thoughts of rebellion, escape, or suicide. As graphically displayed in the popular movie *Amistad*, numerous black captives committed suicide. Clearly, the thought of slavery was unbearable for many of them.

Myths and Stereotypes of African Heritage

Many early anthropological interpretations of Africans and their culture were negative and spoke of the "uncivilized" people. As Molefi Kete Asante, in the book *The Afrocentric Idea*, put it, "Any interpretation of African culture must begin at once to dispense with the notion that, in all things, Europe is the teacher and Africa is the pupil . . . because Western theorists have too often tended to generalize from a Eurocentric base."[6] In short, much early thinking about Africa and its citizens was based on myths and stereotypical assumptions. Whites chronicled the mediocrity of Africans, accepting "the universal law of slavery" set forth by George Fitzhugh, a Virginia lawyer of the 1800s. Fitzhugh propounded a view based on his belief in the natural inequality of man. In this view, numerous stereotypical beliefs about blacks were reinforced. More specifically, the universal law of slavery stated:

> He the Negro is but a grown up child, and must be governed as a child . . . The master occupies toward him the place of parent or guardian . . . He [blacks] would become an insufferable burden to society. Society has the right to prevent this, and can only do so by subjecting him to domestic slavery . . . The Negro race is inferior to the white race, and living in their midst, they would be far outstripped or outwitted in the chaos of free competition. Gradual but certain extermination would be their fate . . . In Africa or the West Indies, he would become idolatrous, savage and cannibal, or be devoured by savages and cannibals. At the

North he would freeze or starve . . . We would remind those who
deprecate and sympathize with Negro slavery, that his slavery
here relieves him from a far more cruel slavery in Africa . . . The
Negro slaves in the South are the happiest, and, in some sense,
the freest people in the world . . . The children and the aged and
infirm work not at all, and yet have all the comforts and neces-
saries of life provided for them . . . The women do little hard
work and are protected from the despotism of their husbands by
their masters . . . The Negro men and stout boys work, on average, in good weather, not more than nine hours a day. The balance of their time is spent in perfect abandon. Besides they have
the Sabbaths and holidays . . . With their faces upturned to the
sun, they can sleep at any hour; and quiet sleep is the greatest of
human enjoyments . . . Tis happiness in itself—and results from
contentment with the present, and confident assurance of the
future . . . [7]

Obviously the stereotypical beliefs behind Fitzhugh's universal law of slavery were inaccurate and based on untruths. In 1914
another example of stereotypical beliefs was provided by J. M.
Mecklin, a renowned white anthropologist who detailed the inferiority of African blacks:

The most striking feature of the African Negro is the low forms of
social organization, the lack of industrial and political cooperation, and consequently the almost absence of social and national
self-consciousness. This, rather than intellectual inferiority,
explains the lack of social sympathy, the presence of such bar-
barous institutions as cannibalism and slavery, the low position
of woman, inefficiency in the industrial and mechanical arts, the
low type of group morals, rudimentary art-sense, lack of race
pride and self assertiveness, and an intellectual and religious life
largely synonymous with fetishism and sorcery. (Herskovits, 59)

More than eighty years ago, two prominent black writers,
W. E. B. DuBois and Carter G. Woodson, along with white anthropologist Melville Herskovits from Northwestern University, began
to dispel some of the early myths and misconceptions of the
African heritage. Specifically, Herskovits challenged many of
Mecklin's assertions and subsequently found that practically every
statement made by Mecklin was incorrect or misleading. For
instance, with regard to the arts (which some Africans may have

engaged in during their free time), Herskovits found evidence that Africans were indeed very instrumental in the development of some of the world's most famous art forms. A typical example is woodworking, the African form of which still influences present-day artists. While woodcarving is one of the most preeminent African arts, Africans were also very proficient in weaving and other arts.

Myths of the African economy were also largely inaccurate. Most early writings suggested that Africans were highly unsophisticated and therefore lacked the intellectual ability to incorporate complex economic systems into the fabric of African society. In reality, in order to longitudinally support rather large populations, the African economy had to be far more intricate than many whites understood. Africa was populous, and to maintain such a large number of people, its societies must have had a degree of orderliness and structural organization. How could such a large population maintain itself without some effective management? To fully understand Africans and African culture requires hours of careful attention, careful looking and listening, a willingness to reject preconceived ideas, and a determination to avoid hasty judgments premised on biased cultural views.

The preslavery play, recreation, and leisure of black Africans, like virtually every other aspect of the African past, has been shrouded in myths and misconceptions. Many early historians depict the recreation and leisure of preslavery Africans as relatively purposeless and simplistic. One of the most consistent myths is that, prior to slavery, Africans were barbaric, with no meaningful recreation or leisure history until the European arrival. In fact, Africans have always been involved in a broad and unique array of recreation and leisure pursuits—especially music, dance, and storytelling.

African Music, Dance, and Folktales: Pre-America

Enslaved Africans brought very little with them from Africa to America. Among the most important play, recreation, and leisure customs they brought were their music and songs, their folktales,

and their dance. Africans have always been interested and proficient in a wide range of recreation and leisure activities. To
understand the authentic music of Africa, one must be willing to
reject the notion that it was "primitive," consisting predomi-
nantly of merely rhythmic noises. When early white European
explorers visited Africa, a virtually unexplored continent, their
impressions of African life were flawed by ignorance and prejudice. This prejudice was fueled because they measured African
culture by European standards, which consistently interpreted
African culture as lacking sophistication.[8]

Africans were proficient in aesthetic expression, most out-
standingly in song. Music has always been an integral part of
African life, from birth till death.[9] Not all Africans were musicians
or singers, but many possessed a unique sense of musical rhythm.
This instinct for musical rhythm not only produced a large number of talented vocalists and percussionists, but also enabled many
Africans to master the techniques of some complicated early
melodic instruments, such as gongs, rattles, zithers, flutes, fiddles,
lutes, harps, bow-lutes, musical bows, miriltons, whistles, the
kakaki, the alghaita, and clarinets.[10]

Although only a relatively small portion of songs performed
with these instruments were transcribed, those songs indicate a
wide range of singing styles accompanying the music. This variety
points to the difficulty of comprehending "African" music under a
single canon. As Herskovits stated:

> It is of some interest to trace the changes in point of view as to the
> origins of Negro music that have taken place in the United States.
> It was first assumed that, in essence, the songs of the Negroes rep-
> resented a welling forth of the anguish experienced under slavery.
> In time, however, opinion grew that, since this music differed
> from other forms of musical expression, Africa was to be looked
> to for an explanation of its essential characteristics.[11]

Herskovits also believed that the complexity of West African
musical forms with respect to scale, rhythm, and general organization, and the many varieties of songs—ranging from lullabies
through work songs, songs of derision, and social dance songs, to
sacred melodies—were as varied as the individuals by whom they
were sung.

Some of the most important individuals responsible for the transmission of African songs, music, traditions, and folktales were the *griots*. Griots were the verbal historians of African society, noted for their ability to remember and recall events. These individuals were skilled poets, musicians, and storytellers. They also offered personal opinions and moral judgments in their performances. Indeed griots were consummate performers.[12] They could not only recall words to songs and remember older African instruments, but could also proficiently perform in the old African traditions. Some griots, like other Africans, had been captured and sold into slavery in America, so even in slavery Africans depended on griots to transmit their traditions, including music, play, recreation, and leisure. Griots would pass on stories of how Africans played in the homeland, what they did for fun, relaxation, entertainment, and enjoyment, and even teach the traditional dances of the homeland.

Dance is another aesthetic leisure form in which Africans excelled. In fact, dance was a fundamental element of African aesthetic expression and could be found everywhere in Africa, in a multitude of forms. At the height of the antebellum period, it was estimated that approximately 85 percent of slaves were natives of West Africa.[13] Europeans who visited West Africa prior to U.S. slavery were amazed at African dance and commented on the many variations found there.

Dance is probably the most obvious physical form of recreation and leisure that Africans brought to the New World. Like the music that Africans enjoyed, the dances they perfected encompassed a wide variety of purposes. There were ritual and recreational dances, religious and secular dances, and fixed or improvised dances. To attempt to specifically describe each of these is beyond the scope of this book, however some specific dances will be described later. These were very prominent in the African culture and in their lives, free time, and ceremonial time—including in the recreation and leisure of the people. African dances were influential in the evolution of modern dance all around the world.

English historians observed and recorded some African dances prior to American slavery. An English writer's observation of a Sierra Leone ring dance in 1721 provided this description:

Dancing is the Diversion of their [black africans] evenings: Men and women make a ring in an open part of the town, and one at a time shews his skills in antick Motions and Gesticulations, yet with a great deal of Agility, the Company making the Muisick by clapping their hands together during the time, helped by louder noise of the two or three Drums made of a hollowed piece of Tree, and covered with Kid-Skin. Sometimes they are all around in a circle laughing, and with uncouth Notes, blame or praise somebody in the Company.[14]

James Barbot, a slave trader who made a number of trips to the African coast, described a dance he observed in Nigeria in the early 1700s:

Their dances are commonly in a round, singing the next thing that occurs, whether sense or nonsense. Some of them stand in the middle of the ring, holding one hand over their head, and the other behind their waist, advancing and strutting out their belly forwards, and beating very hard with their feet on the ground. Others clap their hands to the noise of a kettle, or a calabash fitted for a musical instrument. When young men, or boys, dance with maidens or women, both sides always make an abundance of lascivious gestures; and every now and then each takes a draught of palmwine to encourage the sport.[15]

Barbot and others observed certain unique characteristics of African dance including the circle, the hand clapping, and the stamping of the feet. Although many visitors to Africa described African dance as characteristically high in energy, in truth African dance was complete. It ranged from the very subtle to the most dynamic and sophisticated of movements. Some of these characteristics traveled with the Africans from their homeland to the West Indies and eventually to slave plantations in the United States.

Indeed, Africans truly enjoyed dance. The proficiency with which they danced did not always produce positive outcomes. This excellence in dance led to as a method of capturing Africans. Aside from the most common ways slaves were obtained—by abduction, as prisoners of war, and by purchase from slave dealers—dance was used to entice Africans to board the slave ships. Realizing their pride in their proficient dancing, the crews on slave ships would invite Africans on board to dance, promising food or other rewards. Once on board, they had lost their freedom and were captured, shackled, and eventually taken from their homeland.

As Africans journeyed to America, African dance began a transformation from the traditional proud African dance. It is likely that this transformation started on board slave ships during the journey to America. Slave ships were notoriously overcrowded and disease-ridden, but in order to receive the most profit from the slaves, it was important to keep them in the best possible physical condition. This was a challenge for the profit-hungry slave merchants.

Most slave ships were so crowded that many slaves were forced to sleep lying front-to-back, making it difficult to move. Some captives were positioned with their heads between the legs of other slaves, enduring the foul odors of urine and feces of their brethren. Most male slaves were shackled in chains, but most females were allowed more freedom to roam—though most remained close to the imprisoned males—and were at the mercy of their captors.[16]

In order to exercise the slaves, and sometimes for the entertainment of the crew, their captors would periodically, if infrequently, have them dance. This dance, as the sailors liked to call it, did not demonstrate the vitality and purposefulness of traditional African dance. Forced to obey their tormentors, those in irons were ordered to stand up and make whatever motions they could, and such movements surely did not capture the pure enjoyment associated with traditional African dance. Thus, the transformation of the unique African dance began. And such dancing was encouraged for economic reasons.[17] These movements were used as a basic form of exercise for slaves on board crowded slave ships. This allowance continued until the slaves could be put on the market or until they landed at their eventual destinations.

Notes/References

1. Ira Hutchinson. 1973. *Recreation and Racial Minorities.* In Thomas A. Stein and H. Douglas Sessoms, eds. *Recreation and Special Populations.* Boston: Holbrook Press Inc., 335.

2. Ibid.

3. Charles Johnson and Patricia Smith. 1998. *Africans in America: America's Journey Through Slavery.* New York: Harcourt Brace & Company, 77–96.

4. Molefi Kete Asante and Mark T. Mattson. 1992. *Historical and Cultural Atlas of African-Americans.* New York: Macmillan Publishing Company, 9.

5. Johnson and Smith, 5; Mel Watkins. 1994. *On the Real Side: Laughing, Lying, and Signifying—The Underground Tradition of African-American Humor That*

Transformed American Culture, from Slavery to Richard Pryor. New York: Simon & Schuster, 49.

6. Molefi Kete Asante. 1987. *The Afrocentric Idea.* Philadelphia, PA: Temple University Press, 59.

7. Leslie H. Fishel and Benjamin Quarles. 1967. *The Negro American: A Documentary History.* Glenview, Il: Scott, Foresman and Company, 91–92.

8. Harold Courlander. 1975. *A Treasury of Afro-American Folklore: The Oral Literature, Traditions, Recollections, Legends, Tales, Songs, Religious Beliefs, Customs, Sayings and Humor of the Peoples of African Descent in the Americas.* New York: Crown Publishers, Inc., 2.

9. Francis Bebey. 1975. *African Music: A People's Art.* High Holborn and London, England: George G. Harrap and Co., Ltd., and Lawrence Hill and Co., 8.

10. Ibid., 40–118.

11. Melville Jean Herskovits. 1941. *The Myth of the Negro Past.* Boston: Beacon Press, 262.

12. Watkins, 64–65.

13. LeRoi Jones. 1963. *Blues People: Negro Music in White America.* New York: William Morrow and Co., x..

14. Dena J. Epstein. 1977. *Sinful Tunes and Spirituals: Black Folk Music to the Civil War.* Chicago: University of Illinois Press, 5.

15. Lynne Fauley Emery. 1988. *Black Dance: From 1619 to Today,* 2nd ed. Pennington, NJ: Princeton Book Company, 3.

16. Deborah White. 1999. *Ar'N't I a Woman: Female Slaves in the Plantation South.* New York: W.W. Norton, 19.

17. Emery, 5–9.

Chapter Two

DURING SLAVERY

The Slave Trade

The African slave trade began with the Portuguese exploration of the African coastline shortly after 1400. Portugal's initial aim was to expand trade,[1] and this marked a new era for the Portuguese. This interaction with Africa resulted in a profitable trade in gold, pepper, and ivory, but the chief prize was the fresh labor supply for the newly settled lands across the Atlantic.

By the middle of the sixteenth century, due to increased competition and a growth in influence, the three biggest trading powers were England, Holland, and France. So profitable was the European slave trade that even the Roman Catholic Church entered the business as a grantor of commercial privilege to prevent Christian nations from engaging in wars of access to the African Coast.[2] Usually the church granted an *asiento*, a signed agreement with a slaving nation that ensured the nation's right to a specific region of Africa.

Slave trading was not a simple process. It did not simply involve securing blacks from Africa, transporting them to the Americas to be sold, and making a return journey for more slaves. Sometimes slave ships spent a significant amount of time on the African coastline negotiating with some Africans for other Africans to be sold into slavery.

Once the slaves were acquired, the ships would venture to the West Indies which served as a "seasoning" post, often for as long as three years. There slaves were conditioned for the customs of slavery in America.[3] This seasoning essentially consisted of training blacks for the general requirements of slave labor. Those who survived could eventually be transported to other destinations.

Despite the seasoning process, many captives never made it to America. As many as a hundred million may have died along the way. Some died from disease on board the slave ships, others died at the hands of their captors, some of the more sickly were thrown overboard, and still others died by hurling their bodies into the sea rather than succumb to the drudgery of slavery. Those who survived the voyage across the ocean had more horrors to endure. Once they arrived on the American coast, confused, terrified, and often sick, they might spend as much as two weeks quarantined in "pest houses" on board the ships.

Consequently, the ways that slaves were captured and sold had a significant impact on the continuation of their African cultural heritage,[4] including their play, recreation, and leisure. It is uncertain which and how much African culture and tradition was lost in the process. We know that certain aspects of cultural heritage are lost when people are separated, whether voluntarily or by force, from their culture. The treatment of Africans purposely attempted to separate enslaved blacks from their African heritage. The institution of slavery required slaves to be subservient and dependent which in itself violated their African heritage.

The exact time frame in which this African heritage was dismantled is uncertain. Possibly it began aboard the slave ships when slaves were crowded together with hordes of other unfamiliar victims. Africa is a very large continent with many different cultures and languages. Enslaved blacks, unfamiliar with one another, had to communicate and live with each other. This may have forced many of them to develop new or modified languages, religions, and lifestyles, including recreation and leisure interests and behavior.

The alteration might also have occurred during the passage from Africa to America. Some psychological change would surely take place in the bowels of the slave ships. During the three- to twelve-week passage to America, chained together in detestable conditions of sickness, mania, and disease, many slaves were forced to watch as others were abused for the pleasure of crew members or thrown overboard.

The erosion of African culture could also have happened when they arrived in America at the slave auction, an extremely dehumanizing experience. The following excerpt is perhaps not entirely representative of every slave auction during the entire slavery period, but it offers documentation of the auction experience. At the age of ninety, James Martin, born a slave on a Virginia plantation in 1847, described a slave auction he witnessed:

> The slaves are put in stalls like the pens they use for cattle—a man and his wife with a child on each arm. And there's a curtain, sometimes just a sheet over the front of the stall, so the bidders can't see the "stock" too soon. The overseer's standin' just outside with a big Black snake whip and peperbox pistol in his belt. Across the square a little piece, there's a big platform with steps leadin' to it. Then they pulls up the curtain, and the bidders is crowdin' around. Those in back can't see, so the overseer drives the slave out to the platform, and he tells the ages of the slaves and what they can do. They have White gloves there, and one of the bidders takes a pair of gloves and rubs his fingers over a man's teeth, and says to the overseer, "You call this buck twenty years old? Why there's cut worms in his teeth. He's forty years old, if he's a day." So they knock this buck down for a thousand dollars. They calls the men "bucks" and the women "wenches." When the slaves is on the platform—what they calls the "block"—the overseer yells, "Tom, or Jason show the bidders how you walk." Then, the slave steps across the platform, and the biddin' starts. At these slave auctions, the overseer yells, "Say, you bucks and wenches, get in your hole. Come out here." Then he makes 'em hop, he makes 'em trot, he make 'em jump. "How much," he yells, "for this buck? A thousand? Eleven hundred? Twelve hundred dollars?" Then the bidders makes the offers accordin' to size and build.[5]

Inhumane treatment, often far worse than what Martin describes, was common during the slave auction; it is little wonder that a person's dignity, respect, and proud cultural heritage would be forgotten or diminished

Even the few free blacks were not safe from the slave auction. Due to the exceptional profits of U.S. cotton production, over 200,000 free blacks were captured from their homes in Virginia and sold into the deeper South. So popular was the slave auction that permanent auction houses were built to handle the large volume of sales.[6] The popularity of the auctions would bring slave speculators from all around the country, often days before a slave auction, looking for a good deal. The early slave auctions were probably the first points where blacks began to have an impact on white recreation. In addition to the business conducted, the slave auction was also a time for whites to engage in play, recreation, and leisure. Some whites used the time preceding the auction to drink, socialize, and gamble.

Many speculators and slave buyers were not the most socially refined persons, and they treated their slaves—like the majority of other slaveholders—inhumanely. Such inhumane treatment clearly eroded African pride and tradition and had negative and lasting, potentially irreversible effects on the enslaved. The loss of control and independence associated with such treatment was bound to carry over into the long-term thinking and behavior of enslaved Africans.

The Slavery Period

The period of slavery in the United States was a magnificent yet horrendous era. Anyone interested in obtaining a fuller understanding of modern American racial strife should examine the slavery years. Movies such as Steven Speilberg's *Amistad* generated renewed interest in the institution of slavery, but as we enter a new century both black and white Americans seem weary of constant reminders of the old evils of slavery. Nevertheless, the impact of slavery on many contemporary blacks remains particularly painful. Even the filming of *Amistad* required special sensitivity between blacks and whites, so that only black crewmembers were allowed to put shackles on black actors.[7] That movie was made more than 130 years after emancipation, but Americans, regardless of their color, still desire to understand the realities and impact of slavery on current behavior.

Slave Recreation

It was June 1860. Cato and April were married. They had been allowed to "jump over the stick" some twenty years ago. Their seven children, like themselves, had been born into slavery, so life in bondage was all they knew. Cato, April, and their children were owned by William and Mary Johnson of Jefferson County, Virginia. The Johnsons, like most slave owners, relied on their slaves to work the plantation fields and supply the labor associated with plantation work. The Johnsons worked their slaves six days a week from before dawn to dusk. After the day's work was done, the slaves had little time left for anything except eating and sleeping, which were necessary so the slaves could be ready for work early in the morning of the next day.

All the Johnson slaves worked the required routine or faced the wrath of the slave owner and/or the overseer. The only times slaves had for themselves were Saturday nights and Sundays—if they had put in a good work-week. Slave owners also customarily allowed some holidays, though not for the house slaves. All slaves yearned for these periods of free time.

Cato and April were field slaves who, according to most accounts, worked much harder than house slaves. House slaves worked much closer to the whites, who considered them the lowest form of being, yet most slaves thought it was an honor and a privilege to be a house slave. As field slaves, both of them often working as many as fifteen to nineteen hours a day, Cato and April were physically drained at the end by evening. Since there was little time left for socializing apart from whatever contact they had while working, their lives were generally very monotonous—until Saturday evenings and Sundays (although time off was never guaranteed).

Slaves might socialize and frolic with one another during barn-raisings or corn shuckings, but the work had to be completed before they could have some fun.

For the slaves who had the interest and energy, Saturday evening was the time for real merrymaking. Sometimes slaves from nearby plantations would gather at a designated place for a party that might last into the wee hours of the morning.

When they were younger, Cato and April liked to attend these parties. In fact, they met at a gathering of this type. Slaves liked to dress up, as best they could for these occasions, and Cato and April were no exceptions. "Dressing up" for April simply meant tying a ribbon in her hair. For Cato, it meant borrowing a worn-out hat from a friendly house slave.

The highlight of the party was the dancing. Slaves had to be very careful with what they said and did around their owners, so the party was a time when they could feel free. Even though time was limited and controlled by their masters, slaves played and had fun within those limits. Dancing was a form of self-expression and since most slaves' self-expression had to be curtailed, dancing was a welcome outlet.

Cato and April were two of the best dancers at the slave parties. Their ancestors came from two different African tribes, so the dances they did were distinctly different. Yet when they danced, Cato and April made their moves work well together. When they were on the dance floor, other slaves marveled at how they brought two African dances together to form something unique. They danced fast and they danced slow, while the circle of onlookers cheered them on. They and the others in attendance were about to start another dance when suddenly the door burst open. It was the overseer. The socializing was over for the night.

Sunday was the time for relaxing. Unlike Saturday, when slaves worked most of the day and then had some free time, Sunday was often a whole day of free time. The house slaves were often busy on Sundays attending to their owners, but most field slaves could relax—at least physically. Many slaves spent their Sundays worshipping, visiting other slaves, hunting, fishing, gardening, or just lounging about the slave quarters. Although Cato had to hunt and fish on Sundays to help supplement his family's food supply, he learned to enjoy these activities and sometimes spent hours engaging in them. Sunday was also the time when he had courted April.

The slave period in the United States ran from approximately 1620 to 1865. Of all the periods in American history, the era of slavery is the one most Americans would like to forget. Many whites are afflicted with misunderstanding and denial about the realities of slavery. They find it inconceivable that anyone could have been treated so harshly by their forefathers: One slave boy was forced to whip his naked mother to death, and a young man had to beat his pregnant wife until the baby died.[8] Regardless of their alleged reasons, such punishment is inconceivable. Most whites feel justified in denying their connection to these horrors, because most whites were not slave owners. Yet a large portion of the white population was not initially opposed to slavery.

Still, the nightmares they experienced in slavery did not completely destroy the African heritage.[9] Although a systematic process essentially "trained" men and women into servitude, it is not clear how much African heritage and culture survived. During this period slaves had to develop new, sometimes revised, cultural and leisure behaviors, habits, and attitudes in order to adapt to horrendous life conditions.

Multiple factors had impact on the survival of African culture and its play, recreation, and leisure during slavery. Some of the more important determinants were where the slaves lived, when they were brought to America, and how large a plantation they worked. A new slave, slavemasters theorized, brought memories of their homelands and certain patterns of behavior and attitude to their fellow slaves.[10]

In a more recent account, Ira Berlin's book *Thousands Gone: The First Two Centuries of Slavery in North America* identifies four distinct kinds of slave societies in North America: the Northern colonies, the Chesapeake Bay area, the Carolina low country, and the lower Mississippi valley.[11] Berlin analyzed slavery as far back as the seventeenth and eighteenth centuries. Perhaps one of his most interesting findings was the transitional periods when slavery changed. According to Berlin, these transitional periods encompassed three generations: the "charter generation" brought from western Africa and Europe to the Eastern American coast, the "plantation generation" transported inland to work large estates, and the "revolutionary generation" living in thrall as the democratic ideals of the eighteenth century engulfed them. The lives of

slaves on plantations were by far the grimmest. While each generation deserves attention, the following discussion addresses the
plantation generation.

One of the more salient factors affecting African cultural survival was the size of the plantation on which the slave lived.[12] Most
captured Africans were transported to the West Indies, Brazil, or
North America. In the West Indies and Brazil, slaves were concentrated on large sugar plantations. These plantations needed a great
many slaves, often as many as five hundred slaves per plantation.
In these environments, it was possible for slaves to re-establish
some preslavery African heritage, culture, and tradition. On farms
and plantations with large populations, most field slaves had less
contact with whites. As a result, they did not have to adjust as
much to white culture, language, and religion as they did on
smaller plantations. Indeed, on many large plantations, slaves'
mastery of the English language was far less advanced than on
smaller plantations. On larger plantations slaves might conduct
their own religious celebrations and continue to speak their native
languages, dance native dances, sing native songs, and play native
games, thus maintaining some of their African culture.

In America, plantations tended to be smaller and more scat-
tered, and to employ fewer slaves. Even in the lower South with its
larger slave population the majority of plantations and farms had
fewer than fifty slaves. Only in a limited number of states—including Arkansas, Georgia, Louisiana, Mississippi, and South
Carolina—were there some plantations with more than five hundred slaves. These slaveholdings equated to less than one percent
of the holdings in all states except South Carolina. Slaves on
smaller plantations had much closer working relationships with
their masters. These closer relationships did not imply better treatment or a greater sense of familiarity with their masters.[13] Rather,
it meant that slaves would learn and possibly replicate more of the
masters' behavior and culture.

Again, in order to maintain dominance, whites purposely
diluted much African culture. Slave owners and other whites did
not recognize and accept African slaves as human beings, and they
made few attempts to acculturate them to their new environment.
To ensure that African tradition was not continued, newly
imported slaves were often treated differently than resident slaves.
Later, the slave owner might impose severe sanctions on slaves

found practicing the traditions of their African culture.[14] These punishments alone substantially eliminated much of the African heritage. If the slave owner had the resources and the time, newer slaves would be gradually accustomed to work.[15] They would be distributed in small numbers among the resident slaves so they could acquire the habits of the older slaves and dilute their traditional culture and community.

Nonetheless, there was a sense of community among slaves— old and new, men and women, adults and children. Separated from mainstream society and allowed no opportunity to reap substantial benefits from their new environment, slaves had to operate cooperatively, creatively, and with ingenuity in order to survive culturally and socially.

Not surprisingly, most slaves were only minimally successful in maintaining African culture. Notwithstanding the fact that many slaves on larger plantations were forced to attend church services organized and supervised by whites, most slave communities organized their own church congregations without the approval or involvement of plantation authorities. The church played an important role in transmitting and perpetuating black religious, social, and community beliefs. Slaves from smaller plantations who had insufficient numbers or who were not allowed to congregate for church, yearned for activities that would bring them some contact with fellow slaves from neighboring plantations, bringing a sense of community and African cultural connectedness.

Despite all this, slaves were very resilient. They drew upon the remnants of their African heritage to build and continue a strong cultural heritage, including recreational and leisure traditions. Their African cultural beginnings and traditions had to be modified and sometimes eliminated, but portions of African heritage survived. Two of the more notably lasting African traditions, music and dance, will be discussed later.

Notes/References

1. Leslie H. Fishel and Benjamin Quarles. 1967. *The Negro American: A Documentary History*. Glenview, IL: Scott, Foresman & Co., 4.

2. Molefi Kete Asante and Mark Mattson. 1992. *Historical and Cultural Atlas of African-Americans*. New York: Macmillian Publishing Company, 24–26.

3. Fishel and Quarles, 5.

4. Edward F. Frazier. 1957. *The Negro in the United States,* 2nd ed. New York: Macmillan Publishing Company, 3.

5. George P. Rawick, ed. 1972. *Texas Narratives,* vol. 6, *The American Slave: A Composite Autobiography.* Westport, CT: Greenwood Publishing Group, 62 – 65.

6. Charles Johnson and Patricia Smith. 1998. *Africans in America: America's Journey Through Slavery.* New York: Harcourt Brace & Company, 217, 296–97.

7. D. Ansen and A. Samuels. 1997. "Amistad's Struggle," *Newsweek,* 8 December, 64–67.

8. Johnson and Smith, 340.

9. D. Crowley. 1977. *African Folklore in the New World.* Austin: University of Texas Press, vii; Mel Watkins. 1994. *On the Real Side: Laughing, Lying, and Signifying—The Underground Tradition of African-American Humor That Transformed American Culture, from Slavery to Richard Pryor.* New York: Simon & Schuster, 54–55.

10. Frazier, 8.

11. Ira Berlin. 1998. *Many Thousands Gone: The First Two Centuries of Slavery in North America.* Cambridge, MA: Harvard University Press, 93–215.

12. Frazier, 44–58.

13. David K. Wiggins. 1979. *Sport and Popular Pastimes in the Plantation Community: The Slave Experience.* Ann Arbor, MI: University Microfilms International, 8.

14. Ira Hutchinson. 1983. "Recreation and Racial Minorities." In *Recreation and Special Populations.* Thomas Stein and H. Douglas Sessoms, eds. Newton, MA: Allyn and Bacon, 339.

15. Frazier, 8.

16. T. Webber. 1978. *Deep Like the Rivers: Education in the Slave Quarter Community, 1831–1865.* New York: W.W. Norton & Company, 191.

Chapter Three

THE ANTEBELLUM PERIOD

In order to put more of the black recreation experience into perspective, some mention must be made of whites and recreation during the antebellum years. In the early to mid-1800s, most southern whites lived on plantations or farms. Life on the larger plantations was extremely comfortable, perhaps the most elegant in America. Plantation owners had a reputation for gracious hospitality to their visitors; of course, it was the responsibility of the slaves to see that the needs of visitors were addressed.

Whites—Recreation and Leisure

With so many personal obligations being taken care of by slaves, it would appear that all whites needed to do was recreate. Though more recreation time would eventually come to the slave owners, this was not true at first. In reality most slave owners probably spent far more time working their plantations or seeing that the work was completed than engaging in recreation and leisure. Nevertheless, unlike the labor of blacks, the planters' exertions yielded considerable time for recreation and leisure pursuits. The advent of slavery had given plantation owners and their families precious individual time to develop hobbies, read, engage in politics, write books, hunt, and attend social functions.

Whites lived in both rural and urban areas, and those in urban areas were afforded more recreation opportunity, more refined and varied social activities; and since some of these more refined activities were not available to rural plantation owners, some had their entertainment brought to them. It was not uncommon for plantation owners and their families to be given music and dance lessons in their homes.[1] Obviously such advantages were not offered to the enslaved, so blacks gained no noticeable proficiency in the white modes of music and dance.

Whites also enjoyed public social centers like local taverns. Taverns were important centers of daily life in rural communities, and whites might travel many miles to congregate, talk business, and socialize. There, white men met to talk politics, gamble, drink, play games, read newspapers, socialize, and simply take time away from their everyday work and worries.

Sometimes whites gathered at large functions for group pastimes. At such rural gatherings as barbecues, barn-raisings, log-rollings, hog-killings, and quilting bees, whites engaged in a variety of games and sports. Some of the most popular were throwing the sledge, wrestling, jumping ditches, fives, long bullets, bandy, gander pulling, slow racing, shooting, and horsemanship.[2] Wealthier whites seldom took part in the games, remaining spectators, but they did engage in more sophisticated entertainments of the period including theater-going and giving or attending elegant parties.

Whites, with or without slaves, had more opportunity for leisure pursuits. Even though not all Southerners were slaveholders, economic dependencies, bonds of kinship, personal ambition, and racial solidarity connected the slaveholding class to the lower ranks of southern society. This connectedness remained strong, and whites grew "comfortable and accustomed to slaves providing a carefree way of life."[3] Even the white abolitionists who were generally against slavery often chose to remain silent. The majority of the abolitionists were poor, while the rich whites who owned slaves made the laws. Whites, especially in the Lower South, believed that slavery was a necessity, and even some abolitionists in the Upper South and the North accepted it as a necessary evil in a developing nation.

Free Blacks—Recreation and Leisure

Not all blacks in America, or all those with black lineage, were slaves. In 1810 there were 2,988,132 blacks in America. Of that number, 1,191,362 were slaves and 1,796,770 were free blacks.[4] As the century progressed more blacks gained their freedom. However, the "freedom" was far from the true meaning and spirit of the term. Most free blacks resided in the North. Before the American Revolution, only a few free blacks lived in the South.

Free blacks were not welcome in most places in America, especially the South. Most free blacks were the very light-skinned children of mixed racial unions and were referred to as mulattos. In general, these individuals were freed after serving a designated time of servitude (if their mothers were white) or were manumitted by guilt-ridden white fathers. In the colonial south, only a few free black children descended from wealthy slave-owning whites, and most of them were born of white indentured male servants and black women or of black men and white servant women. Nonetheless, these children were not born free. The law gave masters the services of interracial children for thirty-one years and locked their mothers into additional terms of service.[5]

Even when they were freed at the age of thirty-one, they often found the free world very cruel. Whites, especially southern whites, continued to chip away at their individual rights. Some southern colonies barred free blacks from many privileges of freedom including holding office, voting, serving in the military, testifying against whites in court, and having sexual relations with whites.

Initially, only the right to own property and the freedom to travel freely were not infringed upon. As a result free blacks as compared to slaves, could travel in search of personal and occupational opportunity. However, many whites were suspicious of any free blacks seen traveling and would stop and harass them under the pretense that they were runaway slaves. Consequently, many free blacks, frustrated with this constant harassment, limited their travel, and consequently their recreation and leisure, to their surrounding localities.

Freedom for blacks was essentially a state of mind that carried over into how they felt about themselves as individuals. Not realizing all the liberties associated with the concept of freedom, they were happy just to be free from the mandatory "requirements" of slavery. Freedom was closely connected to recreation and play. In 1645 one newly-freed black man put it this way: "Now I know myne owne ground and I will worke when I please and play when I please."[6] This same longing for freedom was one reason that many slaves ran away from their oppressors. Just to taste freedom, even for a limited time (even an hour, a day, a week, or a month), was something that some would risk the wrath of their masters for.

A limited number of blacks moved from slavery to freedom with relative ease. One group that was sometimes freed was comprised of adults and elderly persons who were handicapped and deemed "past labor," freed because their masters discarded them as no longer valuable. Some better-natured slave owners might emancipate some blacks, but not always for humanitarian reasons. George Washington and Robert Carter were two such men. Both eventually emancipated hundreds of slaves, but first they had to assure other whites that freed blacks would not cause problems or be burdens on their communities. This called for some careful planning. How did Carter manage it?

> Carter awarded small lots to all of his newly emancipated slaves over forty-five, assigning three free men to each lot. He also made special arrangements with his Black foremen, house servants, and others he thought especially trustworthy. In 1792, as his plan of emancipation went into effect, Carter permitted James Bricklayer, George Cooper, Gloucester Billy, Sam Harrison, and Prince to rent houses and garden plots and to hire their wives and children. They were allowed to take firewood from his land, but he insisted that they pay their own tithe. In addition some of those Negroes had to perform their former task without pay. Prince continued to receive and deliver grain, and his son, Harry, took care of Carter's stock as he had before. Besides his new responsibilities as a free man, Sam Harrison had to shave Carter, dress his wig, and do the customary duties in the study.[7]

What was Carter's rationale? Profit. Carter believed that by providing gradual freedom to trustworthy and experienced slaves, he would bring in more profit in the long run. He expected these blacks to hire other former slaves who would eventually hire themselves out to neighboring farmers. Carter was correct in his assumptions, and so began the institution of sharecropping.[8] Nevertheless, such plans were not always fruitful. Many free blacks, after years of repetitive and burdensome slavery, opted not to reinvest their wages in the hard work of sharecropping. Some chose to live what they considered the "high" life. They spent their limited wages on fancy clothes and played the "dandy." Still others celebrated their freedom with long vacations from work. Some, because the connection between slavery and labor was so intimate, chose to spend their free time in idleness. In short, they opted to live off the land and worked only when necessary. This helped to confirm the stereotypical beliefs of many whites about blacks: they were inherently lazy and would work only under rigid direction. However, a close observer will view this behavior as natural, indeed as predictable, after years of servitude. Liberty would be equated with not working.

Further, free blacks had to understand their irreversibly lower social position and remain subservient. In order to retain their freedom, they must adhere to societal laws instituted largely to keep free blacks subservient. For instance, in 1861 in Norfolk, Virginia, black people were forbidden to smoke. If found smoking, they were subject to arrest and, if convicted, were fined or whipped.[9]

Notwithstanding this situation, free blacks began to create new opportunities for themselves. They purchased farms, opened their own shops and businesses, entered occupations formerly closed to them, and founded their own churches. Importantly, it was not freedom that prompted free blacks to form these separate organizations. The development of separate organizations was due to their systematic exclusion from white institutions. Forming their own organizations was not easy. Most lacked both financial capital and organizational experience, and faced white opposition—the most detrimental factor. Many whites believed that if blacks formed their own organizations they might achieve a measure of equality, an idea that most whites found difficult to endure. Philosophically, whites refused to consider themselves equal to a group of persons they despised.

As more blacks gained their freedom, white slave holders grew more and more disturbed. They were convinced that, if slaves saw others of their color similarly enslaved, they would be content. However, if they saw other blacks enjoying all the rights and privileges of freedom, they might rebel. Whites' fears were intensified as free blacks purchased property, built churches and schools, and established a sense of identity as free people.[10] In the long run, many whites began to see blacks becoming more like them and were infuriated.

The color of the free person had a lot to do with white attitudes to freedom. Initially, whites were more willing to allow freedom to lighter-skinned free blacks, but as darker-skinned blacks were freed, whites reconsidered the status of free blacks. Especially in the South, free blacks began to see their civil rights limited, their economic opportunities restrained, and their mobility curtailed. Essentially all that remained was the right to hold and defend property.[11]

Imposed travel limitations controlled the economic opportunities of the freemen and severely affected their recreation and leisure. As more blacks gained their freedom, white slaveholders feared the corruption these freemen would bring to their slaves and spearheaded efforts to have free blacks relocated to other areas. When blacks gained their freedom, most opted to relocate to the North or to larger urban areas where there were larger numbers of free blacks. Because of travel limitations, most became city dwellers, and their recreation and leisure were confined to the urban locale.

Those free blacks who stayed in rural areas found life very challenging because whites mandated that they could be employed only in certain occupations, primarily those involving manual labor. Ira Berlin, chronicling the life of free blacks, observed that for no more than the signing of a contract with the promise of food, clothing, and shelter, hundreds of free blacks sold their services for periods as long as twenty years,[12] thus resigning themselves to a state of near-slavery. Although most free blacks avoided such contracts, many had to contract by the year, which left them still bound to a white master. These contracts, drawn up by slave holders, specified that free blacks must work according to the rules governing slaves. In some instances they could not leave the plantation during the contract period and they had to work when and as the slaves did. In short, while legally free, their freedom, including their recreation and leisure, was severely curtailed by white slave holders.

Many free blacks asserted their independence and boosted their self-esteem by refusing to work under these conditions. Some decided it was best to live off the land, so to speak, and not to work, so they were perceived as lazy. Despite this, some became entrepreneurs and developed their own businesses. Usually, they ran small businesses like boarding houses, restaurants, and grocery stores.

This, too, had a significant impact on black recreation. Many of these businesses doubled as saloons and gambling houses where free blacks, slaves (on Saturday afternoons and evenings, Sundays, or holidays), and occasionally whites gathered for play, recreation, and leisure. These establishments were especially needed in a society that provided very little recreation and leisure for non-whites. This was one of the first relatively organized recreation and leisure activities outside the plantation for blacks in America. Free blacks were establishing their own recreation and leisure pursuits.

Slaves—Recreation and Leisure

Slaves were relegated to the lowest level of American society. Most whites viewed them in the most negative stereotypical terms as ignorant, emotional, dirty, clownish, loyal, and childlike. Many whites even believed that slaves were not total human beings, and—conveniently for slave owners, that they could and should be worked hard and given very little in the form of comfort.[13] Scholars and analysts who study slavery focus on the more obvious realities of slave life: slave-master relationships, management of slaves, slave laws, slave punishment, work periods, slave religion, slave family relationships, etc. Although each of these is important to an understanding of slave life, there is a void in the area of what slaves did during non-work time. Slaves did not simply eat, work, sleep (although these did encompass most of a slave's life), and continually repeat this cycle. It is true that slaves had very few spare hours, and they spent much of that time trying to survive by cultivating gardens or raising poultry.

Nevertheless, what slaves did during non-work hours was a major determinant of the remainder of their lives. Without some meaning to the non-work time, a slave's life would quickly become unbearable; and the institution of slavery would collapse.

Their toil was difficult and required much stamina. The plantation work of slaves was generally concentrated in two primary agricultural areas: rice and cotton, both of which required significant manual labor. The cultivation of rice, began in the late 1600s, made plantation owners wealthy.[14] Initially knowing little about rice cultivation, the owners turned the work over to slaves. Rice is a thirsty crop that requires early and thoughtful preparation to secure a successful planting season. Beginning in the spring, slaves prepared the land inch by inch with hand-held hoes because the wet soil could trap horses and plows. Not all the land was wet enough, so slaves often had to divert streams or build dams to create water reserves for the rice fields. This required long hours of ditch-digging in addition to the harvesting and preparation of the crop for distribution.[15]

When rice lost its appeal, cotton became the crop of choice for the southern plantation owner. Like growing rice, cotton planting and cultivation required long hours of manual labor. Cotton then demanded the almost never-ending handwork of cleaning. What's more, this work had to be completed in some of the hottest weather. Slaves worked the hot fields to cultivate the cotton in addition to completing other plantation and farm work, survived the cold winters with limited clothing, and often endured poor and insufficient diets. Food, clothing, and shelter, then, constituted the most basic necessities, but the limited amusements, pleasures, and privileges were also important.

Most of the slaves' recreation and socialization was done among other slaves in their close surroundings. Amusements were simple and privileges few and far between, but they were highly cherished by the slaves. As constructs, recreation and leisure imply components of personal control and autonomy that can hardly be applied to a slave. Considering all this, one might ask whether slaves had any "true" recreation or leisure.

To the slave master, slavery was a business matter. Slaves had to be made obedient, respectful, and subservient. They were taught to feel inferior, though their masters also attempted to instill the belief that slaves stood to profit by being respectful, cheerful, submissive, and hard-working. Profit might mean a better job and less harsh physical and mental treatment, but no privileges were guaranteed.

In the effort to better regulate slave behavior, masters often encouraged them to be jovial and festive. Even as they worked tirelessly, slaves were expected to sing and display an air of contentment and merriment. Often slave owners used such performances as entertainment for themselves and their guests. It is not difficult to imagine a couple of slave owners sitting in the shade of a porch with cool glasses of water, watching slaves sing and hum as they performed difficult plantation work.

Slave narratives continuously illustrate that the masters were better pleased with slaves who were not sullen and who displayed happiness. A silent slave presented a greater threat to the overseer because the master could not discern what he or she was thinking. Even during their limited leisure time, slave behavior was observed with fascination by whites. The slaves who appeared happiest increased in value, could be sold more easily, and would bring a better price.

Slave Humor

Under these dismal conditions, slaves used their wit in their recreation, entertainment, and leisure. Blacks gained proficiency at a number of word games and verbal contests. One such activity was known as *signifying*. Signifying is commonly described as putting down or berating another individual with witty comments and is also referred to as ranking, sounding, or *dissin*. *Mother rhyming* or *the dozens*, as they were called, in which one mocks or ridicules another person or her/his relatives, were also forms of entertainment. This type of verbal play has been traced to a number of African tribal groups, including the Efik, Dogon, Yoruba, and some Bantu tribes.[16] This joking aggression called for a special kind of humor and quick wit in which Africans excelled.

Obviously, even when engaging in these verbal contests, slaves were not entirely free in their word choice. They had more freedom in speaking about themselves in the company of other slaves. William Schechter, an early speculator on slave behavior, observed that slaves were allowed to openly criticize and kid themselves, without fear of punishment, but when speaking of whites, they had to be very subtle. When slaves did speak in the presence of, or about, whites, they had to be cautious and witty, underlaying their humor with a secondary meaning.[17]

Schechter's analysis illustrates the importance of viewpoint in interpreting slave behavior. Depending on one's viewpoint or perspective, slave behavior might suggest different analytical conclusions. W.E.B. Du Bois describes this viewpoint in *The Souls of Black Folk* where he alludes to a double consciousness of blacks. Du Bois describes the unique sensation of consistently perceiving oneself through the eyes of others which epitomizes the double identity of the slave. This double identity was necessary for survival. As Du Bois puts it "One ever feels his twoness—an American, a Negro; two souls, two thoughts, two unreconciled strivings; two warring ideals in one dark body, whose dogged strength alone keeps it from being torn asunder."[18]

Richard Wright in *Black Boy* came closest to describing this phenomenon as he recalled the advice given to him by an older black teen: "When you're in front of white people, think before you act, think before you speak. Your way of doing things is alright among our people, but not for White people."[19] Frederick Douglass also describes it accurately in his autobiography when he conjectures that the slave's seemingly joking Sambo-like behavior did not portray the slave's true state of mind.[20] The Sambo role slaves undertook was the most submissive personality. While acting Sambo, slaves appeared to be in total agreement with their masters. Anything said by the master was okay and not to be questioned. These behavioral adjustments required slaves to assume dual social roles: one for the hostile world where they interacted with whites, and another for their more relaxed and natural interactions with other slaves.

Slave Codes

One of the most consistent ways to govern slave rights and behavior was through the initiation of slave codes. On one level, slave codes were developed as a means of controlling the activities and behavior of blacks. On another level, slave codes were initiated to outlaw virtually all preslavery customs. These codes or laws governing behavior affected every aspect of the slave's life.

The southern colonies had the most highly developed codes governing blacks, severely restricting even free blacks. In 1712 South Carolina passed "An Act for the better ordering and governing of Negroes and Slaves."[21] This comprehensive measure served as a model for other slave codes in the South. These codes had far-reaching effects. It was unlawful for blacks to be disrespectful to whites; to trespass on a white's property; to raise horses, cattle, hogs, or sheep of their own; to leave the plantation without a written pass or certificate of freedom; to play any games of cards or dice; to play any game of chance, hazard, or skill for any money, liquor, or other kind of property; and to go armed or hunt with a gun. It was also unlawful for anyone—black or white—to teach or attempt to teach a slave or free black to read or write.

Codes varied from plantation to plantation, region to region, state to state, and addressed other wide-ranging restrictions on blacks, many of which had a definite impact on black recreation by limiting travel, marriage, gambling, education, legal lawsuits, language, and crimes against whites. In general slave codes forbade slaves to leave the plantation without passes or in groups without a white person present; forbade assembling at night without a white person present; set curfew times; forbade carrying firearms unless with written consent of masters; etc. In theory, these codes also carried responsibilities for slave masters including requiring them to hide guns from blacks; identifying the days slaves could come to the cities and listing permissible reasons for such trips; and advocating public whippings, jail, and/or death for blacks who violated specific local ordinances. However, in actual fact most municipalities were reluctant to place too many restrictions on what a slave owner could do with his or her "property."

As slave codes were not official laws, there was a wide variance in the treatment and expectations of slaves from plantation to plantation. Most often the treatment was determined by such factors as the disposition of the master or overseer, the disposition of the slave, the type of plantation worked, and the work load of slaves. The disposition of the slave could have a major impact on his or her treatment by the slave master. Some slaves, overwhelmed and sensing the futility of any real resistance, probably survived by becoming what is known as "Uncle Toms" or "Sambos." Blacks needed to play the role of the jovial, loyal, and congenial slave in order to survive. This meant using cunning and deceit (Du Bois's twoness) when dealing with their white masters. Although many modern blacks consider this behavior intolerable, the slave *had* to develop techniques of deception. Such mechanisms called for feigning ineptitude and ignorance.

Variations in Slaves' Recreation and Leisure

An adult slave's day was very structured. Much of the freedom we currently attribute to leisure was nonexistent. Even slaves who spent the majority of their lives on only one or two plantations were constantly forced to alter their personal attitudes and behaviors simply to survive. In most instances, the amount of free time allotted was based on the slave's occupation.

Each kind of slave had a different amount of free time. In the emerging nation, most slaves worked in rural areas, but there were some urban slaves in manufacturing jobs, on the railroads, and shipping docks, and in numerous other occupations.[22] Here we focus on the plantations where there were essentially three types of slaves: field slaves, house slaves, and skilled slaves.

Generally, no laws governed the amount of time a slave could work. In some southern states—for example, Georgia and Alabama—it was legal to work slaves for *nineteen hours a day*,[23] and as a result some slaves died. For the most part, however, slaves worked about fourteen hours a day, six days a week in fall and winter, and approximately fifteen hours a day in the growing seasons.[24] This was not due to compassion, but to the reality that slave owners were trying to buy slave loyalty and also trying to convince their captives that their lot was improving—not to mention keeping them healthy enough to work hard.

During slavery, recreation or leisure time was thought to be whenever the slave was not working. However, one must rest and sleep in order to work the following day, so there was little time for true voluntary recreation or leisure as they are currently defined.

Most slaves on plantations were field slaves. They were assigned the most physically difficult work. A typical field slave began the workday before sunrise, preparing breakfast and feeding livestock. Throughout the remainder of the day, depending on the season, they would be planting or picking cotton and other crops, cutting trees, building ditches, clearing land, hoeing fields, and building fences.

House slaves, on the other hand, had a different routine. Sometimes working as personal servants, they were often envied by other slaves. They were thought to be better off in terms of material comforts. They ate better food and had better clothing (discards from the slave owner and his family), and their work was typically not so physically demanding. However, their work hours were less predictable and they could be called on at any hour of the day or night. Most house slaves were females whose duties included cooking, serving meals, sewing clothes, working gardens, cleaning house, caring for livestock, supervising children, washing dishes, attending to the needs of houseguests, drawing baths, setting tables, laying out clothes for the day, and running personal errands.[25]

Skilled slaves, like house slaves, also held more privileged positions, especially in wealthier plantation communities. Along with plantation work, these slaves labored as blacksmiths, carpenters, stonemasons, millers, shoemakers, horse trainers, and in other trades. The major differences between skilled slaves and other slaves were that they were not consistently under the supervision of whites, had better opportunities to earn money, were allowed to leave the plantation more frequently, and—most important probably—had some limited control over their work time. Having somewhat more flexible work schedules, they had more, and probably more independent, free time.

It became traditional to grant later portions of Saturday evenings, Sundays, and certain holidays as days off for the slaves. House slaves, however, were not consistently granted these non-work periods. Indeed, it was during such times that they were busiest, often staying up late to prepare for the next day's events.[26] The master might entertain guests on Saturdays, Sundays, and holidays, and it was important that these guests be properly attended to. That was part of the house slaves' job.

Time Off from Work

The brief time off from the daily drudgery was allotted only because of the presumed profit it would bring to the slave owner in the long run[27] and because it was virtually impossible for the masters to oversee their slaves every hour of the day. They required time for their own lives, including for recreation and leisure pursuits. Free time, then, was not offered because of an inherent interest in the slave's quality of life, but those few hours, in addition to the comfort of religion, provided a modicum of happiness amid the sufferings of slavery.

Many slave owners felt that granting free time helped build a "society at home" which would decrease the problem of runaway slaves. What's more, such breaks maintained the health of the slaves, making them stronger workers. Some cunning masters provided so much alcohol on holidays that slaves suffered miserable hangovers and couldn't wait to get back to their regular routines. Other masters took seriously the Christian tradition of granting non-work days, and still others saw festivities as a means of averting rebellions.[28]

The slave's workload varied with the season of the year. Some might receive time off during the summer if it was "unusually" hot and humid. Some might be given about two hours of free time in the middle of the day to rest and prepare to work later. In any case, time off from work was clearly not provided for leisure's sake; rather, it was provided to make slaves more productive. Slaves might also be given time off during inclement weather, on very rainy or cold days, but masters might instead find other chores for them, including cutting and stacking wood, cleaning houses and cabins, shoveling, shucking corn, etc. Bad weather for the slave also meant bad weather for the master, who did not want to work or supervise under those conditions. This meant slaves had time to sleep, socialize, sing, or simply lounge around their quarters.

Since slaves were totally at the mercy of people who did not think that they deserved human rights and privileges, why were they allowed *any* free-time? Frederick Douglass was convinced that the granting of leisure time on holidays and Sundays was allowed primarily for the purpose of social control. Douglass believed that holidays were effective means of keeping down the spirit of rebellion among the slaves, something many whites deeply feared. Essentially, holidays—with alcohol occasionally provided by the masters—kept the slaves' minds on the immediate pleasures of singing, dancing, eating, and drinking. If not for these, Douglass thought, the rigors of bondage would become too severe to endure, and slave revolt would be more commonplace.

Sometimes slaves got time off for other reasons. Some were granted special non-work periods for displaying "appropriate" behavior. In other words, if a slave consistently pleased the master, he or she could expect some free time. Some slaves, primarily the highly skilled, were assigned particular tasks to perform and did not have to work in gangs. If a skilled slave finished a task early, he or she had free time.[29]

The most important feature of free time for the slave was simply the freedom from work, a significantly valued freedom that produced great satisfaction. Slave work was hard, and any deviation from this obligation was cherished.

Due to their life circumstances, some slaves took the significant risk of running away.[30] They ran away for a number of reasons: anger over other family members being sold, fear of overseers and slave owners, slave-owner relocation, and sexual abuse by slave owners. Being sold, of course, had a definite impact on slave recreation. When individuals are disconnected from their immediate surroundings and loved ones—which could happen any time to slaves—there tends to be a certain amount of tension, apprehension, and worry. Accordingly, when such separation occurred, slaves were forced to separate from their pasts and make a connection with the present. What was acceptable play behavior or recreation in one setting might not be suitable or acceptable in another.

While many slaves ran away intending never to return, the most common form of absconding was closer to "truancy" or "absenteeism." In these cases, slaves would leave for short periods of time, sometimes for recreation. In addition to visiting displaced family members, many absconded to hunt, fish, consume whisky, and hide from the drudgery of the work routine. Others ran away to visit members of the opposite sex or visit local dance halls, or to play cards at local establishments.[31] Such absenteeism, although risky and with potentially life-threatening consequences, often increased the limited happiness of slaves.

Another important factor in the slaves' happiness was that free time was less supervised than work time.[32] For those in bondage, free time broke some of the monotony of daily toil under constant supervision. Finally, during free time, slaves could take out some of their anger toward their masters by engaging in physical contests, worshipping, or singing songs of bondage. These activities allowed slaves to vent their frustrations against their masters without actually rebelling. Rebellion carried severe penalties.

One of the most important values of slave recreation and leisure is that it led to cultural formation through cooperation, social cohesion, and tighter communal bonds. In effect, slaves formed strong and lasting bonds during their participation in recreation and leisure. It provided some assurance that one need not lose all mental balance under the demands of slavery. Slaves needed some time in which they could find some happiness in their otherwise dreary lives. Had it not been for these brief periods of recreation and leisure, slaves might not have survived the institution of slavery at all.

Nevertheless, even during non-work time, slave owners continually attempted to shape the attitudes and behaviors of their slaves. Slaves' recreation time was often restricted by slave owners' rules. Slaves were usually granted free time only on the home plantation so that whites could continually monitor them. Eventually, whites developed specific legislation to limit slave mobility, as we have already noted.

What did slaves do during their free time? They slept, lounged, sang, socialized, and told stories. Adult slaves were especially proficient in singing and storytelling. Through their songs and tales, blacks communicated about the drudgery of slavery, past lives in Africa, and their hope for a brighter future. Slave songs were an essential medium through which all sorts of information was transmitted, both positive and negative. Many whites saw slave singing as evidence of contentment and happiness. Nothing could have been further from the truth. Frederick Douglass was one of the first to explode this myth.[33] Douglass recalled that as a slave he often sang to drown his sorrow, but seldom to express happiness. Crying for joy and singing for joy were uncommon while he was in the jaws of slavery.[34] W. E. B Du Bois also explained the nature of slave songs in his classic book *The Souls of Black Folk* and wrote,

> What are these songs, and what do they mean? I know little of music and can say nothing in technical phrase, but I know something of men, and knowing them, I know that those songs are the articulate message of the slave to the world . . . They are the

music of an unhappy people, of the children of disappointment;
they tell of death and suffering and unvoiced longing toward a
truer world, of misty wanderings and hidden ways.[35]

Whites, from as far back as the time of Thomas Jefferson, had
high regard for the singing ability of slaves. Some went so far as to
imply that blacks were natural singers and musicians. Obviously,
though race has little to do with natural music ability, many agree
that blacks have been blessed with musical ability. One reason
slaves perfected their musical talents might be that music was one
of the activities they were most free to engage in. In their music,
slaves engaged in widespread exchanges and even picked up some
of the music of the whites around whom they lived. Yet, throughout the centuries of slavery and even long after emancipation, their
songs retained characteristic and improvisational styles closer to
that of West Africa and South America than to the musical styles of
Western Europe and white Americans.[36]

For the most part, specific African songs were not retained
throughout the slavery period. Slaves came from a number of different African communities with different songs, languages, and
traditions. As slaves in America they were more or less required to
develop communities uniquely their own. Yet they continued to
utilize music in much the same way as their African ancestors had.
Music remained a central, living element in their daily expression
and activities. In slavery blacks sometimes timed their work routines to the tempo of music, much as their African ancestors had.
They had frequent recourse to their music, and they used it in
almost every conceivable setting for almost every conceivable purpose. There were songs of satire, children's songs, nonsense songs,
lullabies, work songs, and songs of play and love.

Some slaves utilized musical instruments brought with them
from Africa like the banjo, the musical bow, several stringed instruments, and a number of percussion instruments. In America, they
learned to play the guitar, violin, and other instruments common
to the Europeans. Some played the instruments primarily for their
own pleasure and that of fellow slaves. However, proficiency with
instruments could have additional rewards. Slave owners sometimes used musically talented slaves for their own enjoyment and
entertainment, and these slaves were allowed some of the same
extra privileges accorded to house slaves and skilled slaves.

Traditional Times for Play, Recreation, and Leisure

Generally slaves were provided time off from work on Saturday
afternoons or evenings, Sundays, and select traditional holidays,
which included the Fourth of July, Christmas, Thanksgiving,
Easter Sunday, and New Year's Day. Collectively this adds up to
about fifty-seven periods per year when slaves could—almost—
count on time off from the usual drudgery. Due to the rarity and
irregularity of free time, slaves longed for these periods. Like ordinary nights after a day's work had been completed, these periods
were generally provided for rest, not for the enjoyment of play,
recreation, or leisure. Nonetheless, once the slave owner had designated these days as non-work days, they were expected by the
slaves, who were generally free to engage in activities for their
own enjoyment. Slave owners very rarely prohibited their slaves
from celebrating because it might increase the danger of disobe-
dience and rebellion which the owners and other whites feared.

Fifty-seven periods of time may not appear an unreasonable
amount of time for play, recreation, and leisure. However, even
during these times, slaves had to take care of all their duties which
were not work-related, including washing, cleaning, maintaining
family relationships, providing additional food for the family,
sleeping, going to church, resting, and recuperating from the previous period's labor.

SATURDAY AFTERNOON AND EVENING

Depending on the disposition of the slave owner, the work week
ended on Saturday afternoon or evening, provided that the brunt
of the week's or day's work was accomplished. Some especially
cruel slave owners were reluctant to grant even these modest
respites from mandatory work, but they were not the majority.
Eventually tradition extended these opportunities for free-time
activities such as lounging about the cabin or plantation, fishing,
and addressing family business. Over time, some slaves might
even have their own parties, or the master might provide some
forms of amusement.[37]

In the slave quarters, activities could often be engaged in away
from the view of the overseer. Since the average work week lasted
six days, activity in the slave quarters on Saturday evenings and
Sundays was cherished.[38] In a sense, the plantation slave commu-

nity was built around the slave quarters.

The slave narratives include numerous accounts of Saturday nights as times for frolicking, dancing, and partying until a signal from the "big house" announced that it was time to retire. Sometimes overseers would lock cabin doors and institute a patrol system to keep the slaves in their quarters.

Saturday afternoons or evenings were also times when more generous masters gave their slaves passes to legally leave the plantation and visit surrounding plantations and cities. This custom was not favored by all whites. In fact, the old custom of white women keeping off the streets on Saturday afternoons and evenings was initiated because slaves were likely to be on the streets at these times. Slave passes were written permissions that slaves were required to carry when traveling off the home plantation.

As their movements became more restricted, slaves' recreation and leisure focused more on activities available in close proximity to the home plantation. Although Saturday afternoons and evenings were traditionally the free times allotted to slaves, under particular circumstances some might be allowed more time off. The age and health of the slave were the major determinants in these allowances. Slaves who were old and deemed physically unable to complete the required work would be allowed more time off. Many slave owners, however, considered the old slave more a burden than an asset, so the fate of frail and elderly slaves was uncertain. In some cases, they were given meager rations and physically separated from the rest of the slaves to live out their remaining days in isolation and to hope that they would die quickly.[39]

Sometimes when a slave was sick, an allowance of time off might be granted. If there was a chance of such allowance being approved, some slaves took advantage of the situation and became proficient at feigning illness. However, for the most part, slave owners were not quick to make such allowances, and many slaves perished because they were seriously ill but got no time off from the work routine. Given their poor living conditions and lack of adequate medical care, slaves were very prone to sickness. If they did not get adequate rest, they often died performing their duties. Some slave women with multiple children, usually six or more, might be allowed all Saturday to themselves and their children. The rationale was that slave children were, in the long run, profitable for the slave owner. Allowing the slave mother to spend time with her children helped to induce overall cooperation.[40] Some slave women used Saturdays, especially the afternoons, for doing their laundry, which also offered an opportunity to talk and socialize with other women. As slaves aged and their overall energy diminished, they liked to spend their free time with one another. Many nights were spent around a cabin fire, gossiping and telling stories.[41]

For the majority of the young adult slaves who bore the brunt of the heavy work, Saturday nights were chances to socialize and dance. Dancing held a special place in the life of the slave. It was one of the activities, although modified to the circumstances of slavery, they had brought with them from Africa. It was also a means of self-expression, and, it was something the slave could do better than the master. It was a source of great pride for the slaves to be proficient in dance. Most whites, as noted earlier, considered blacks to be forever jolly, so the slaves took pride in finding fun and happiness, no matter what treatment they received from their masters.

Along with dancing, Saturday nights were a time for socializing and partying. Sometimes masters supplied a fiddle and some liquor. Dock Wilborn, a 95-year-old former slave, recalled his master arranging amusements. Dock recalled his master, after the cultivation of the crops was complete in late summer, bringing his fiddle down to the slave quarters and saying that he (the master) would make the music and he wanted to see his "niggers" dance. So the slaves danced for hours to the delight of the master and for their own amusement.[42] How could a slave not dance if the master asked?

Slaves from neighboring plantations might attend these parties, particularly if their masters did not allow them to have parties of their own. Some slave masters were opposed to neighboring slaves attending parties and social gatherings on their plantations for fear of the corruption outsider slaves might bring in. Many slaves were also reluctant to venture far from their home plantations for fear of white patrols, which were frequently unsympathetic to any black caught off the home plantation and which might inflict severe punishment on those apprehended.

Whites attempted to control the dancing, partying, and drinking of slaves in other ways. An Act of 1794 made it unlawful to permit slaves to dance and drink on another's plantation premises without the written permission of their owners.[43] However, this act was difficult to enforce. Slave parties were one of the major reasons that plantation masters instituted slave patrols to provide surveillance on roads between plantations and to check slave cabins for curfew violations.

In addition to parties and dancing, many slaves gathered on Saturday nights just to make social contact with other slaves. This social contact tended to be outside the view of the master. At these gatherings slaves often told stories which were useful and beneficial in establishing black culture. For one thing, slaves could feel momentarily superior, or at least equal, to their masters by speaking honestly of their daily feelings. As entertainment and morale enhancement, storytelling and folk tales were distillations of folk wisdom, devices to teach young slaves how to survive. A projection of the slaves' personal experience, dreams, and hopes, the tales allowed them to express hostility to the master, to poke fun at themselves, and to delineate the workings of the plantation system. At the same time, slaves could preserve a culture that whites couldn't totally control.[44]

Through their stories slaves often relayed messages of the hope of eventual freedom. One such tale was *"How Nehemiah Got Free."* In this tale, a slave named Nehemiah gained his freedom, outsmarting his mean owner by making him laugh.[45] It was astonishing that slaves developed and told such stories, especially considering the conditions under which they were not allowed to speak their native languages nor to read or write.

THE CONTINUATION OF MUSIC AND DANCE UNDER SLAVERY

Music and songs continued to be principal forms of leisure, recreation, entertainment, and enjoyment for blacks. John Wesley Work, in his book *Folk Tales of the American Negro*, captures the importance of music and songs for blacks in slavery:

> In the Negro's own mind his music held, and still holds, positions of variable importance. In the darkness of bondage, it was his light; in the morn of his freedom, it was his darkness; but as the day advances, and he is being gradually lifted up into a higher life, it is not only his proud heritage but support and powerful inspiration. The songs of the slave were his sweet consolation and his messages to heaven, bearing sorrow, pain, joy,

prayer, and adoration. Undisturbed and unafraid, he could always unburden his heart in those simple songs pregnant with faith, hope, and love. The man, though a slave, produced the song, and the song, in turn, produced a better man. The slave is perennially praised for his perfect devotion. Some attribute it to one cause, some to another. Some even go as far as to attribute it to the influence of the system of slavery, but more than any other cause, the retroactive power of his music influenced the character of the slave. What else could he who had such ideals ever before him? How could a man be base who looked ever to the hills? Could a man cherish the idea of rapine whose soul was ever singing these songs of love, patience and God? Neither African heathenism nor American slavery could wholly extinguish that spark of idealism, set aglow by the creator. This idealism, expressed in terms so beautiful and strong, grew in power, and the possessor found himself irresistibly drawn and willingly striving to attain it. The creator of these songs had now become the creature of his own creation.[46]

Music, songs, and dance continued as fixtures of African cultural heritage, and were practically impossible to dismantle through the institution of slavery. While slave owners took virtually all material possessions from their slaves, it was more difficult to destroy the music, songs, and dance they carried within their souls. Through these mechanisms slaves could express feelings about their predicament and pass these feelings from generation to generation.

Many African cultural traditions were conducted out of sight of whites or when slaves were engaging in their work routines. In these endeavors, slaves were considered the most nonthreatening, so more African traditions were allowed and limited rudiments of African heritage could be maintained. As a result of continued yet limited engagement in these activities and their limited exposure to others, blacks remained proficient in these expressive forms of recreation and leisure, while incrementally revising African traditions.

In some localities slaves continued their African traditions. Initially, more music and dance may have survived in the deeper South in places like Louisiana than in other states. For example, in New Orleans in 1817 the city council voted to provide a special place for slaves to dance. John Blassingame, slave trader and noted observer of slave life, wrote about slave activity in Louisiana, "twenty different dancing groups . . . collected together to perform their worship after a manner of their country. They have their own national music. . . ."[47]

Some specific African customs prevailed in Louisiana. In 1819 one of the better descriptions of African dance (though probably inadequately evaluated) was offered by Benjamin Lathrop, a famous architect. Lathrop saw about five hundred slaves dancing in groups around older men who beat drums, stringed instruments, and calabashes. The men and women danced in separate groups while singing in response to their leaders. Lathrop wrote, "A man sung an uncouth song to the dancing which I suppose was in some African language, for it was not French, and the women screamed a detestable burther on a single note. The allowed amusements of Sunday have, it seems, perpetuated here those of Africa . . ."[48]

Similarly, historian Christian Schultz made the following observation:

> . . . twenty different dancing groups of the wretched Africans, collected together to perform their worship after the manner in their country. They have their own national music, consisting for the most part of a long kind of narrow drum of various sizes, from two to eight feet in length, three or four of which make a band. The principal dancers or leaders are dressed in a variety of wild or savage fashions, always ornamented with a number of tails of the smaller wild animals. . . . These amusements continue until sunset, when one or two of the city patrole show themselves with their cutlasses, and the crowds immediately disperse.[49]

One traveler who arrived in New Orleans after slavery, documented the persistence of these dance rituals in Louisiana:

> Yes, I have seen them dance; but they danced the Congo and sang purely African song to the accompaniment of a drygoods box beaten with sticks or bones and a drum made of stretching a skin over a flour barrel. . . . There are no harmonies—only a furious contretemps. As far as the dance—in which the women do not take their feet off the ground—it is lascivious as is possible. The men dance very differently, like savages, leaping into the air. . . .[50]

African dances and songs were also observed in other areas of the antebellum South, including Mississippi, North Carolina, Florida, and Virginia. It seems these aesthetic forms were so ingrained in the psyche of the slaves that no matter what the consequences they persisted as a form of free-time activity.

Dance was one of last of the cultural traits affected by the move from Africa to America. Most blacks transported from Africa brought few if any possessions with them, but dancing couldn't be totally destroyed by the horror of slavery. Dance manifested itself in the fields while people worked, in the churches where they worshipped, in large plantation gatherings, and in the ring shouts that helped camouflage escapes. Dancing and singing allowed the slave to communicate feelings that couldn't be spoken. Through dance, slaves maintained traditions from a homeland across the ocean. While slaves often learned such dances of whites as the reel, the waltz, and the quadrille, their own dance style remained distinctive.

African dance heritage was even more evident, yesterday and today, in the West Indies. The West Indies was often a seasoning post where slaves were trained into servitude and many Africans were quickly sold into slavery in the Caribbean. The French and Spanish slave owners were more liberal than Americans in allowing Africans to retain elements of their own culture, including dance. This liberty came from the influence of the Catholic Church, not from the good will of the slave owners. Harold Courlander, an early observer, commented, "The Church did not insist on washing out of the African mind everything that was there. The Catholic Church regarded every slave, as a complete and finished man except for salvation."[51]

Thus, in the West Indies slaves were considered more human than they were in America. As a result, more remnants of traditional African dance survived, including the Calenda, Chica, and Juba.

Nevertheless, much of these dance traditions made it to America in varying forms. The large integration of slaves from the West Indies into the United States brought elements of the West Indian dance to American blacks.

> Consider the Calenda: The dancers are arranged in two lines, facing each other, the men on one side and the women on the other. Those who are tired of dancing form a circle with the spectators around the dancers and the drums. The ablest person sings

> a song which he composes on the spot on any subject he con-
> siders appropriate. The refrain of this song is sung by everyone
> and is accompanied by great handclapping. As for the dancers,
> they hold their arms a little like someone playing castagnettes.
> They jump, make swift turns, approach each other to a distance
> of two or three feet then draw back with the beat of the drum
> until the sound of the drum brings them together again to strike
> their thighs together, that is, the men's against the women's. To
> see them it would seem that they were striking each others bel-
> lies although it is only their thighs which receive the blows. At
> the proper time they withdraw with a pirouette, only to begin
> again the same movement with absolutely lascivious gestures;
> this, as many times as the drums give the signal, which is many
> times in a row. From time to time they lock arms and make sev-
> eral revolutions always slapping their thighs together and kissing
> each other.[52]

Although the dance was modified in different geographic
regions, the Calenda, according to most accounts, had certain basic
characteristics: it was performed by one or more couples encircled
by a singing, clapping ring; the movement of a couple consisted of
a type of shuffling advance and retreat, with most of the movement originating in the hips, while the limbs played a minor role.
Except for the description given by Labat, there was no physical
contact between the dancers. Even though the Calenda—also
known as the Kalenda, the Jo-and-Johnny, and the
Calenda—[53] was considered vulgar and distasteful by some, it
proved to be among the slaves' favorite pastimes.[54]

The Chica was another popular dance that reached the
American mainland, especially the New Orleans area. According to
St. Mery:

> When one wants to dance the Chica, a tune, especially reserved
> for that type of dance, is played on crude instruments. The beat
> is very pronounced. For the woman, who holds the ends of a ker-
> chief or the sides of her skirt, the art of the dance consists mainly
> of moving the lower parts of her loins while maintaining the
> upper part of her body practically immobile. Should one want to
> enliven the Chica, a man approaches the woman while she is
> dancing, and, throwing himself forward precipitously, he falls in
> with the rhythm, almost touching her, drawing back, lunging
> again, seeming to want to coax her to surrender to the passion

which engulfs them. When the Chica reaches its most impressive stage, there is in the gestures and in the movements of the two dancers a harmony which is more easily imagined than described.[55]

Very much like the Calenda, the main characteristic of the Chica was the rotation of the hips with an immobile upper body. It further appears that the role of the woman was that of flirtation while the man pursued and enticed.

The Juba or Jumba was essentially a competitive dance of skill. In this dance:

> Presently a woman advances and commencing a slow dance, made up of shuffling of the feet and various contortions of the body; thus challenges a rival from among the men. One of these, bolder than the rest, after a while steps out, and the two then strive which shall first tire the other; the woman perform- ing many feats which the man attempts to rival, often excelling them, amid the shouts of the rest. A woman will sometimes drive two or three successive beaux from the ring, yielding her place at length to some impatient belle, who has been mean- while looking on with envy at her success. Sometimes a sturdy fellow will keep the field for a long time, and one after another of the other sex will advance to the contest only to be defeated; each one, as she retires, being greeted by the laughter of the spectators.[56]

A number of other dances with African origins were main- tained throughout the years of slavery, but, the dance of American slaves was influenced by the absence of the drum for musical accompaniment. This lack was primarily the result of the 1739 Cato conspiracy or Stono insurrection in South Carolina. In the early eighteenth century the slave population grew considerably, creating concerns about slave revolt. The brutal conditions of slav- ery provoked a number of rebellions and uprisings known as the Cato Conspiracy and the Stono insurrection led to the imposition of strict regulations regarding the use of drums by blacks.

This most serious rebellion occurred on a plantation in Stono, South Carolina. The Stono insurrectionists killed guards, secured ammunition, joined other slaves, and proceeded to Florida, marching to the sound of drums. Consequently, after the rebellion nervous whites forbade blacks to use drums in any form, even for recreation and leisure.

Without drums for musical accompaniment, dance nevertheless persisted. The cakewalk, which had its roots in West African festivals, was reportedly one of the most common dances performed during plantation celebrations. The dance was sometimes performed at the end of a harvest, and the plantation owner would offer a cake to the winning couple[57] (The dance often involved competition for such prizes). In this dance slaves formed a circle in whose center one couple after another would promenade and prance, sometimes with buckets of water on their heads, sashaying and high-kicking to the music of banjos and hand-clapping. The dance itself had numerous variations, and was viewed by the slaves as a slightly veiled humorous caricature of their masters' pretentious posturing and pompous attitudes.[58] In short, slaves used portions of the dance to make fun of whites.

The cakewalk, initially known as the "chalk line walk", was popular until the early part of the twentieth century. At first, there was little prancing, just a straight walk as, turning here and there, dancers made their way with pails of water on their heads. The winning couple was the one that remained most erect and spilled the least water. Later the dance grew more elegant, the pail of water was eliminated and replaced with more fluid and graceful movements. Later, blacks continued to dance the cakewalk in professional vaudeville performances. Eventually, in some vaudeville acts the professionals would offer prizes to the best local couples performing the cakewalk. As a result, the dance continued to spread and became one of the blacks' most popular dances.

So popular was the cakewalk that the dance spread quickly and fanned out from the black community to white America. As whites began to do the cakewalk, they made subtle changes in the dance. Prior to the end of the nineteenth century, white American dance was very controlled, patterned, and formal, with limited body movement and contact.[59] Through the initiation of the cakewalk and other dances, whites learned to move more fluidly.

Other very popular slave dances were the Ring Dances and the Buzzard Lope. The Buzzard Lope consisted of an elaborate pantomime enacting the walk and pecking movements of a buzzard feeding off carrion.[60] It has been traced to the natives of Dahomey in West Africa. The Ring Dance or Ring Shout[61] was another popular slave dance with African origins, and was one of the more primitive dances performed on the plantation. It had its beginnings in West African religious ceremonies and involved the whole body, hands, feet, belly, and hips. Slaves formed a ring or circle and proceeded with a half-shuffle, half-stamp accompanied by exaggerated pelvic swaying. The dance was performed by individuals rather than couples, typically at night in slave cabins with everyone involved in the dance. This African dance survived by accident. The Baptist religion would not allow drumming or dancing in the church, but the definition of dancing included "crossing the legs". Since the Ring Dance was performed to hand-clapping with a shuffling step, it was acceptable.

The Ring Shout was generally performed by black Baptists and Methodists. In one of the earliest discussions of black dance and music, Charles Lyell, another observer of slave dance, commented:

> Of dancing and music the negroes are passionately fond. On the Hopeton plantation above twenty violins have been silenced by the Methodist missionaries, yet it is notorious that the slaves were not given to drink or intemperance in their merry-makings. At the Methodist prayer-meetings, they are permitted to move around rapidly in a ring, joining hands in token of brotherly love, presenting first the right hand and then the left, in which maneuver, I am told, they sometimes contrive to take enough exercise to serve as a substitute for the dance, it being in fact, a kind of spiritual boulanger, while the singing of psalms, in and out of the chapel, compensates in no small degree for the songs they have been required to renounce.[62]

The Ring Shout allowed slaves to remain close to two things they loved most: the church and dancing. The Shout became a religious dance of the slaves. H. G. Spaulding, another early observer of slave dance, wrote this description of the Ring Shout:

> Three or four (Negroes), standing still, clapping their hands and beating time with their feet, commence singing in unison one of the peculiar shout melodies, while the others walk around in a ring, in single file, joining also in the song. Soon those in the ring leave off their singing, the others keeping it up while with increased vigor, and strike into the shout step, observing most accurate time with the music. This step is something halfway

between a shuffle and a dance, as difficult for the uninitiated person to describe as to imitate. At the end of each stanza of the song the dancers stop short with a single stamp on the last note, and then, putting the other foot forward, proceed through the next verse. They will often dance to the same song for twenty or thirty minutes, once or twice, perhaps, varying the monotony of their movement by walking for a little while and joining in the singing. The physical exertion, which is really great, as the dance calls into play nearly every muscle of the body, seems never to weary them in the least, and they frequently keep up a shout for hours, resting only for brief intervals between the different songs.[63]

Indeed dancing, generally no matter when or how, was fun for slaves. In addition to being a form of exercise for the slave or of entertainment for the slave master, dancing was pleasurable. However, not all white slave owners encouraged their slaves to dance. In fact, some of them, particularly white southern Methodist ministers, implored their slave congregations to give up the sinful practice of dancing. For the white southern Methodist, dancing was a wicked amusement. Despite such religious opposition, dancing was too popular to be discontinued.

SUNDAYS

Sundays were the slaves' most common time off. Although the practice was not mandatory, Sunday was by custom and tradition similar to Saturday evenings. Some slave owners attempted to control what slaves did on these days. The religious South was much to blame for this. Many slaves belonged to "Christian" masters who were continually reminded by southern ministers of their Christian duties as slave masters. A basic Christian duty was to observe the Sabbath and to keep it holy with religious worship. So slave masters were urged by the clergy not to work their slaves on Sundays. Most slave owners agreed, and the tradition of no work on the Sabbath was born.

As Sunday was a day when slaves expected not to work, they might, if given passes by their owners, congregate in local cities and socialize with one another. Eventually, cities suffered the extra burden of an abnormal accumulation of slaves. For whites this was an undesirable consequence of the non-work Sunday tradition. Since the majority of slaves were plantation workers, many townspeople did not welcome these outsiders. Indeed, in some villages and towns, local authorities frequently tried to clear the streets of blacks on Sundays.[64] In Fayetteville, North Carolina, in 1797 the city commissioners directed local policemen to "flog" with as many as fifteen lashes "Negroes, that shall make noise or assemble in a riotous manner in any streets on the Sabbath day; or they may be seen playing ball on that day."[65] This rule was difficult to enforce, as it required much vigilance on the part of authorities. The laws were not written clearly, so authorities were left to their own discretion in interpreting what was or was not legal. At various times legislators attempted to design laws restricting the movement of slaves on special occasions, but the general assemblies of most states consistently refused to interfere with the rights of masters and of local communities in this respect.

Although unwelcome in most cities, many slaves looked forward to Sundays when they were exempt from ordinary plantation jobs and could make some independent choices in their free time,[66] engaging in a broad array of activities: hunting, fishing, gambling, singing, competing in athletic contests, telling stories, visiting, playing marbles, or attending religious services.

Church activity was especially important. There were few places where slaves felt at ease, and the black church was such a haven. It was in church that the slave felt most at ease. In the old black churches on the plantations, people of African ancestry could express themselves independent of outside white interference. Some slave-owners forbade their slaves to perform some of their more vivacious traditional dances, in church. However, they were free to engage in "dances of the spirit." "Dance of the spirit" was probably one of the first "true" dances. Individuals could abandon themselves to the manifestation of the Spirit of God, moving practically every part of the body to the rhythm of the religious music.[67]

Nonetheless, some masters wanted to curtail these typical Sunday amusements and required their slaves to observe Sunday as a religious holiday and to engage in more sedimentary pursuits. Most such attempts by slave owners to control Sunday activity was unsuccessful. They simply lacked the manpower to supervise the slaves on non-workdays.[68]

HOLIDAYS

In addition to Sundays, most slaves were given time off on selected holidays.[69] Christmas, in particular, was a spirited time for slaves because their masters might extend the Christmas holiday to include more days off, depending on the disposition of the master and the condition of the crop.[70] Typically during the Christmas holidays, slaves had more freedom than at any other time of the year, sometimes three or four days of rest between Christmas and New Year's Day or till "Old Christmas."[71] During the Christmas holidays, some masters were also more liberal in issuing passes so slaves could go into towns or travel to visit relatives, friends, or even former masters. For the most part, however, slaves remained close to home.

"WORK-THEN-PLAY" ACTIVITIES PROVIDED BY SLAVE OWNERS

Many of the social activities slaves enjoyed were significantly influenced by local customs and by the type of work performed on the plantation: corn-shuckings, log-rollings, hog-killings, and quilting bees.[72] For the most part, these work-then-play activities were provided by the masters, so they could hardly be viewed as true leisure. Nonetheless, many slaves recalled the pleasures of these gatherings. It was time away from their typical toil and it allowed an opportunity to socialize with fellow slaves outside the conventional work environment.

Although such get-togethers seemed to be elaborate social functions, in reality the masters were getting more work done by their slaves. The work was camouflaged as fun and generally involved a large number of slaves. Occasionally masters permitted neighboring slaves to gather at one plantation to complete or accomplish a large job more quickly. At 108 years of age, former slave Eliza Washington, recalled corn-shuckings:

> The biggest time I remember on the plantations was corn shucking time. Plenty of corn was brought in from the cribs and strowed along where everybody could get at it freely. Then they would all get corn and shuck it until near time to quit. The corn shucking was always done at night, and only as much corn as

they thought would be shucked was brought from the cribs. Just before they got through, they (the slaves) would begin to sing. Some of the songs were pitiful and sad. When they got through shucking, they would hunt up the boss. He would run and hide just before. If they found him, two big men would take him up on their shoulders and carry him all around the grounds while they sang.[73]

Some corn-shuckings ended with a party or barbecue with food, whiskey, and dancing for the slaves. A former slave, eighty-six year old Campbell Armstrong, described the gaiety during a corn-shucking: "The boys used to just get down and raise a holler and shuck that corn. Man, they had fun. They sure liked to go to those corn shuckings. They danced and went on. They'd [whites] give 'em whiskey too."[74] Another former slave reported,

> They had barbecues. That's where the barbecues started from, I reckon, from the barbecues among the slaves. They would have corn shuckings. They would have a whole lot of corn to shuck, and they would give the corn shucking and the barbecue together. They would shuck as many as four hundred bushels of corn in a night. Sometimes, they would race one another. So you know that they must have been some shucking done. I don't know that I know of anything else [referring to recreation for slaves]. People were ignorant in those days and didn't have many amusements.[75]

Another activity of this type was log-rolling. Log-rollings were also disguised as social activities. If a plantation owner wanted a home built or some land cleared, he invited neighboring plantation owners and their slaves to a log-rolling. In these events slaves often competed to see who could complete the job fastest. Usually after the log-rolling was over, plantation owners arranged a big barbecue or similar meal for the slaves and allowed dancing, and sometimes drinking. Clearly, the social opportunities, in addition to time away from daily work, made these occasions enjoyable.

Not all large social gatherings ended in celebration. During some gatherings slave-holders used slaves as dancers, boxers, wrestlers, and runners for their own and their guests' entertainment and enjoyment. Slaves who performed thus for their masters did not necessarily enjoy the role, but their proficiency did enhance what might be considered a privileged position in the plantation community. Slaves who were proficient entertainers for their owners might be given extra rest time or a lighter workload. As for many performers today, a talent for sports or entertainment was a means to a better life.

Sometimes, slaves sang to entertain whites on Sundays. Abby Lindsay, a former Arkansas slave, at age 84 recalled:

> "I remember white folks used to make the slaves all come around in the yard and sing every Sunday. I can't remember any of the songs straight through. I can just remember them in spots. . . They could go to parties too, but when they went to them or to anything else, they had to have a pass. When they went to a party the most they did was to play the fiddle and dance. They had corn huskings every Friday night, and they ground the meal every Saturday. The corn husking was the same as fun. They didn't serve anything at the corn huskings or at the parties. Sometimes they would give a picnic, and they would kill a hog for that.[76]

HUNTING AND FISHING

Some of the slaves' free time was spent hunting and fishing.[77] Time spent at these activities made some slaves proficient in them. Slaves opted for these pursuits for very different reasons than their masters did. Slave-owners wanted to be considered gentlemanly, and these activities were viewed as leisure sports suitable for men of property. The food—fish and game—obtained was merely a bonus for these white men. Slaves, on the other hand, hunted and fished as a matter of survival, to supply their families with a more varied food supply than was offered by the slave owner. Some slaves, would have eaten no meat for months at a time, if not for hunting.[78]

Some slaves of course, brought their skills at hunting and fishing with them from Africa. Others learned by observing their masters, who sometimes took them along as workers, trappers, and cooks. In some cases, instead of using dogs to scare out prey, slave owners sent slaves into a swamp or wilderness area to frighten animals out into the open. In this capacity, the slaves became much more skilled hunters than their masters simply in order to outwit the wild animals who might otherwise attack them.

Most southern laws restricted slaves' right to hunt without whites, because whites did not want slaves to possess guns. Until 1831 a master could obtain a license for a slave to carry a gun to provide the plantation with game or to kill crows and any other birds destructive to the crops. It was, however, unlawful for a slave to own a gun or any weapon, or to hunt with a gun in the woods. The penalty for violating this law was twenty-five lashes. Hunting by slaves may also have been prohibited because whites considered hunting a gentleman's sport requiring great skill—and thus unsuitable for slaves.

Despite legal restrictions, some slave owners let certain slaves hunt on their land, especially if they shared a portion of the catch. In most instances this permission was given only to older and highly trusted slaves. Rarely allowed to use guns while hunting, slaves became experts at hunting without the use of firearms and at trapping. Many slaves hunted with plantation dogs at night and in other non-work hours. During their free time, slaves hunted squirrels, possums, deer, rabbits, turkeys, and just about anything else they could catch to supplement their food supply. Eventually, whites became uncomfortable having slaves and dogs in the woods at night and restricted this practice.

Slaves also enjoyed and became proficient at fishing. Fishing was one of the most relaxing pursuits a slave could be involved in. Many were as skillful at fishing as at hunting, (so skillful, in fact, that whites began complaining that slaves monopolized all the fishing holes). They utilized a number of methods, including setting hooks, netting, and setting basket traps.[79] Most of these methods were useful because they could be left unattended and required little maintenance while plantation work was being performed.

Whether dancing, hunting, or fishing were considered leisure or recreation for slaves depended on whether they were engaged in for slaves's pleasure or for the master's benefit.

The Play of Slave Children

For some slave children play, recreation, or leisure time was not significantly affected by the conditions of slavery. Generally, the younger the child, the less he or she was burdened with work. There were economic reasons behind this, and it did not mean that masters thought children should play and be happy. Some slave owners did not work slave children too hard because they wanted them to grow up big and strong and become productive and hard-working adult slaves, bringing more financial revenue to their owner.

The lives of most slave children changed drastically and significantly when they became old enough, big enough, and strong enough—generally between twelve and sixteen years of age—to join their fellow slaves in plantation work. Up until this time most children were fairly free to engage in typical childhood activities, sometimes having most of the day free.[80] However, under some masters slave children might be required to work much earlier.

Perhaps this can be better understood through the stories of former slaves. Henry Johnson recounted his experience:

> When I was a little bit a fellow, I used to pack water to twenty-five and thirty men in one field, den go back to de house and bring enough water for breakfast de next morning. When I got a little bigger, I had to take a little hoe and dig weeds out of the crop. If our White boss see a little grass we overlooked he would handcuff our feet to a whipping post, den chain the slave around de stomach to de post and strap de chin over the top of de post and place your hands and feet in front of you. In de start de slave has been stripped naked, and lashed, often to death.[81]

Arkansas former slave Clara Walker, was 111 years old when she reported,

> When I was a girl we skip rope and play high-spy [I Spy]. All we had to do was sweep the yard an go after de cows an' de pigs an de sheep. An' dat was fun, cause dey was lots of us chillun an we all did it together. When I was 13 years old my ol' mistress put me wid a doctor who learned me how to be a midwife. Dat cause so many women on de plantation was catchin' babies.[82]

Indeed, many slave children were required to work to earn their keep. Children, sometimes younger than six years old, performed a number of regular work-related tasks. One young girl recalled having to keep watch over the crop or livestock on the plantation by chasing away crows and keeping the animals from tramping through the plantation fields. Other youngsters weeded, gathered wood, and plucked caterpillars from plants for six days each week.[83]

While their parents toiled in the fields under the hot sun, most children were essentially left alone to play and raise each other. The older children cared for the younger ones and for themselves. They might also perform some non-routine jobs such as carrying water to field slaves, cleaning yards, fetching wood, tending gardens, and feeding livestock. They were sometimes permitted to roam the fields and play basically unrestricted, while the younger children usually had to play in more confined areas, such as yards. Some older children were even allowed to visit other slave children on neighboring plantations, with the stipulation that they return before nightfall. Children on smaller plantations were especially anxious to make these excursions, since it might be their only chance to play with peers of the same age.

Sometimes slave children were allowed to play with white children. Generally, black and white children loved playing together, but on some plantations this was forbidden. Most often it was the slave owner who objected to the children playing together. They did not want their white children corrupted, attitudinally and behaviorally, by slave children. However, as a general rule this practice was hard to enforce, and some black and white children played together in secrecy.

In their play with white children, slave children sometimes received some education, perhaps learning to count. In addition, they picked up traditional American children's games such as shooting marbles, jumping rope, throwing horseshoes, playing hopscotch or mumblety-peg, and jumping poles.

Many slave children recalled being happy to play with white children, but others were not so pleased. Especially for older slave children, playing with white children could be humiliating, as it was not uncommon for a white child to *own* a slave child. For example, at the age of eleven George Washington owned slaves left to him by his father.[84] Following in the footsteps of their parents, older white children were anxious to assume their positions as superiors and to impose their power over the slave children during play. It was difficult to play with another child who "owned" you. Minnie Davis, a slave from Georgia, recalled: "The Crawford children would use me for the doll, and then when my turn came to play mamma and claim one of them for my doll, Miss Fanny or

Miss Sue would appear and then I would have to be the doll for them." Many white children liked nothing better than to torment the slave children and even adult slaves through their imaginative play. Candis Goodwin, a slave in Virginia, remembered that the white and slave children would play Yankees and Confederates. Goodwin commented that the white children were always the Confederates and they would take the black children prisoners and make believe they were going to cut their throats.[85]

When slave children played among themselves, they had to be more creative due to the lack of play materials and equipment. They became efficient improvisers, often developing and naming their own games and activities. Some improvised games included *Smut, Sheep Meat, Once Over,* and *Skeeting.*

In Smut the children used grains of corn instead of cards and called them hearts, spades, clubs, or diamonds, using spots on the corn to identify the card suits.[86] The children also played a modified version of dodge ball called Sheep Meat, wherein a yarn ball was thrown and the child it hit was out of the game. Once Over also employed a ball, or a yarn-ball with a sock around it. This was thrown over the cabin or house to children on the other side. If the ball was caught by a player on the other side, that player ran around the cabin and attempted to hit one of the other team's players, thus knocking him or her out of the game. Skeeting was played in the winter. Children would run, jump on the ice, and skeet (slide) as far as they could—and then skeet some more.

In playing some games, slave children probably learned the basic elements of counting. The many versions of hide-and-seek or old hundred required counting while other children hid. In order to play some of these games, white children taught slave children to count.

Perhaps because they were not allowed to be formally educated, slave children often kept their minds sharp through involvement in intellectual games like riddles. William Henry Towns, an Alabama slave, recalled the following riddle recited by slave children:

> Slick as a mole, Black as coal,
> Got a great long tail like a thunder hole [A skillet]
>
> Crooked as a rainbow, teeth like a cat,

> Guess all of your life but you can't guess that. (A blackberry
>   bush).[87]

There is evidence to suggest that some of the slave children's games came from their African heritage. One such game was Hen and Hawk, in which the chicks line up behind the mother hen who protects them from the hawk or old witch. The hen says:

> Chickname, chickname, chimecrow,
> I went to de well to wash my toe;
> When I came back my chick was gone.
> What o'clock ol' witch?

A colloquy between the hen and the hawk follows:

> Hawk: Hen, give me a chick
> Hen: Hawk, I can't giv' you a chick
> Hawk: I shall have a chick.
> Hen: You shan't have none.[88]

Many of the children's games were cooperative in nature. The majority of these games did not have specific names and were generally called "ring games." In ring games the children often joined hands or formed circles, singing and spinning around. Much like the games of many black children today, particularly those living in large metropolitan areas, these were accompanied by a variety of songs and riddles. The children would typically make a circle and chant, sing, and/or dance to different rhythmic melodies. Participation in ring games continued throughout adolescence, but for the most part ring games were children's games, passed from older children to the younger ones.

For slave children, there was minimal categorization of masculine or feminine play activities.[89] As the children began to grow older, ring games were often the opportunities for youngsters to learn how to interact with the opposite sex and to assume gender roles. Two such games were Peep Squirrel and King William Was King George's Son. In Peep Squirrel a boy and a girl stand some distance apart, facing each other. A different girl gets behind the boy and a different boy lines up behind the girl. The rest of the children sing the following lines while performers suit the action to the words:

Peep, squirrel, eedle, deedle, deedle, dum
Walk around, squirrel, eedle, deedle, deedledum,
Hop along squirrel, eedle, deedle, deedledum,
Skip along squirrel, eedle, deedle, deedledum,
Run the squirrel, eedle, deedle, deedledum,
Catch that squirrel, eedle, deedle, deedledum.[90]

If the boy finally caught the girl (squirrel) he was entitled to a kiss.

In King William Was King George's Son, the children formed a ring around one child and sang:

King William was King George's Son,
And up from the royal race he sprung;
Upon his breast he wore a star,
Three gold rings and a glittering crown.
Go choose the East, go choose the West,
Go choose the one that you love the best.
If he's not there to take your part,
Choose another one with all your heart.
Down on this carpet you shall kneel,
Jes shorz de grass grows in the fiel'.
Salute your bride and kiss her sweet,
Rise again to your feet.[91]

The game would then repeat itself, the boy or girl choosing another to stand in the middle.

Another of the most popular and enduring ring games was Little Sally Walker.

Little Sally Walker,
Sittin' in a saucer
Cryin' for the old man
To come for a dollar
Ride, Sally, ride.
Put your han's on your hips,
Let your backbone slip,
Shake it to the East,
Skake it to the West,
Shake it to the one that you love the best.[92]

Through some of their play, slave children were better able to understand the world around them. A significant amount of their play involved challenging, role-playing, or reenacting events that were significant to them—as does the play of all children. However, the play of slave children presented some distinguishing features. First, they did not always reenact or reflect events found most enjoyable by adult slaves. Second, they usually imitated the social events of their own people and not those of whites (probably due to the general resentment slaves felt towards whites). One such ring game's song went:

My old mistress promised me,
Before she dies she would set me free,
Now she's dead and gone to hell
I hope the devil will burn her well.[93]

Slave children also tried to relieve particular anxieties and fears through their play. One ring game was played by children forming a circle around one child in the middle, who tries to break out of the circle, singing:

Oh, do let me out! I'z in this lady's gyarden,
Oh, do let me out! I'z in this lady's gyarden.

De gate iz locked, an' de wall iz high,
Roun' dis lady's gyarden. *Chorus.*

De gate oz lockt, an' de key iz lo',
Un dis lady's gyarden. *Chorus.*

I mus', I will, git out er here,
Out er dis lady's gyarden. *Chorus.*

I'll break my neck but I'll get out er here,
Out er dis lady's gyarden. *Chorus.*[94]

During this game the children in the circle danced around in time to the music while the child in the middle tried to escape by creeping under, jumping over, or breaking through the walls of the garden (the children's locked hands and arms).

Another ring game was Good Old Egg-Bread. The leader shouted one line and the other children shouted the next. The rhythm was strong and the children stamped their feet very energetically as they circled:

Did you go to the henhouse?
  Yes, ma'am!
Did you get any eggs?
  Yes. ma'am!
Did you put them in bread
  Yes, ma'am!
Did you stir it 'roun'?
  Yes, ma'am!
Did you bake it brown?
  Yes, ma'am!
Did you hand it 'roun'?
  Yes ma'am!

Good old egg-bread,
  Shake 'em, shake 'em!
Good old egg-bread,
  Shake 'em, shake 'em!

Did you go to the lynchin?
  Yes, ma'am!
Did they lynch that man?
  Yes, ma'am!
Did the man cry?
  Yes, ma'am!
How did he cry?
  Baa, baa!
How did he cry?
  Baa, baa!

Did you go to the wedding?
  Yes, ma'am!
Did you get any wine?
  Yes, ma'am!
Did you get any cake?
  Yes, ma'am!

How did it taste?
  So good!
How did it taste?
  So good!
Good old egg-bread,
  Shake 'em, shake 'em!
Good old egg-bread,
  Shake 'em, shake 'em!
Bow, Mr. Blackbird, bow, Mr. Cow.
Bow, Mr. Blackbird, bow no mo'! [95]

Slave children were also influenced by some of the songs they heard their elders singing. Generally sung at night when the adult slaves were resting in their cabins, some of these songs left lasting impressions on the children. One such song "Run, Nigger, Run" went:

Run Nigger, Run; de patter-roller catch you;
Run Nigger, Run, it's almost day.

Run Nigger, Run, de patter-roller catch you;
Run Nigger, Run, and try to get away.

Dat nigger run, he run his best,
Stuck his head in a hornet's nest,
Jumped de fence and run fru de paster;
White man run, but nigger run faster.

Dat nigger run, dat nigger flew,
Dat nigger tore his shirt in two.

Please Mr. Patteroll,
Don't ketch me!
Just take dat nigger
What's behind dat tree.[96]

Some slaves believed that whites made up the song in order to help keep them in line and to induce fears of running away. Whatever the case, many children heard this song all their lives. As a result, the older children allowed to visit neighboring plantations in the daytime were not as terrified of the "patrols" as were the adults. Children traveling unescorted by whites, if they encountered the patrols, were usually simply sent home—though often not nicely.

Slave children also enjoyed role-playing. Some of their games may have been played as ways of coping with some of their greatest fears—whippings and evil spirits—while others were ways of modeling the behavior of adult slaves. In Hide-the-Switch, a switch was hidden and the child who found it ran after the others, trying to hit them. In No Bogey-Man Tonight, one child pretended to be a spirit or the devil and attempted to catch the others.[97]

Anna Woods, a slave from Brinkley, Arkansas, was eighty-six years old when she recalled,

> Yes ma'am, we children played. I remember that the grown folks used to have church—out behind the old shed. They'd shout and they'd sing. We children didn't know what it all meant. But every Monday morning we'd get up and make a play house in an old wagon bed—and we'd shout and sing too. We didn't know what it meant, or what we was suppose to be doing. We just aped our elders.[98]

Sometimes the children played religion and pretended to baptize one another or preach sermons.[99]

Many slave children witnessed the beatings and whippings of their parents and other adults, which significantly influenced their play. Through their play children reenacted some of these practices for a number of possible reasons. One primary reason may have been that it prepared them for the realities of their adult future. In effect, the children were learning how blacks expected to be treated. They were also graphically expressing their innermost feelings and emotions.

Sometimes slave children practiced the roles they would eventually assume by "playing like grown-ups." Girls would dress up like their mothers and pretend to do their mothers' work while the boys refined their singing abilities and practiced whittling, basket-weaving, and other adult male activities.[100] When play got boring, children sometimes watched the adults work, unconsciously gathering information about their own adult lives.

Like the adults, slave children were sometimes forced to play and sing for their masters and their guests.

They also competed in physically challenging activities, such as baseball and marbles, though baseball was not played as it is today. Slave children had no access to traditional baseball equipment and were not privy to the official rules. For example, simply getting a stick and hitting a ball as far as you could was one version of the game, as it would be played on city streets in the early twentieth century.

Overall, there were few organized amusements for slave children. As seventy-two-year-old former slave James Henry Stith put it,

> There weren't many amusements in slave times. They had dances with fiddle music. There was mighty few darkies [who] could get out to go to dances because the patroles was so bad after them. I don't know of any other amusements the slaves had. They were playing baseball when I was born. There were boys much older than I was already playing baseball when I was old enough to notice, so I think they must have known about it in slave time. They didn't play much in that way because they didn't have time.[101]

While games were primarily children's activities, adult slaves also played games, usually to become closer to their children or to relieve boredom. Many slaves recounted uneventful non-work time. Whites did very little to provide recreation or social activities for adult slaves, and some were not even allowed to attend church or Sunday school during their time off. They might simply sit around the plantation since they needed passes in order to leave. Former slave Columbus Williams, recounted at ninety-six that, "The black people never had no amusement. They would have an old fiddle—something like that. That was all the music I ever seen. Sometimes they would ring up and play 'round in the yard."[102]

In summary, for slave children the overall required work coupled with the insensitivity of white slave owners and the lack of family stability assisted in the erosion of quality childhood growth and development. From the beginning, slave children began a struggle in which their overall quality of life, even their play development, was severely restricted.

Notes/References

1. Edward Ball. 1998. *Slaves in the Family.* New York: Ballantine Books, 101.

2. Guion G. Johnson. *Ante-Bellum North Carolina.* Chapel Hill: University of North Carolina Press, 109–112.

3. Charles Johnson and Patricia Smith. 1998. *Africans in America: America's Journey Through Slavery.* New York: Harcourt Brace & Company, 204.

4. U.S. Department of Commerce, Bureau of the Census. 1975. *Historical Statistics of the United States: Colonial Times to 1970,* Part 1. Washington, DC: U.S. Government Printing Office: 14.

5. Ira Berlin. 1974. *Slaves Without Masters: The Free Negro in the Antebellum South.* New York: New York Press, 6–7.

6. Johnson and Smith, 38.

7. Berlin, 59.

8. Ibid., 382.

9. Adele Logan Alexander. 1999. *Homelands and Waterways: The American Journey of the Bond Family, 1846–1926.* New York: Pantheon Books, 127–28.

10. Berlin, 89–90.

11. Ibid., 91.

12. Ibid., 223.

13. Alexander, 98.

14. Ball, 102–105.

15. Ibid., 104–105.

16. Mel Watkins. 1994. *On the Real Side: Laughing, Lying, and Signifying—The Underground Tradition of African-American Humor That Transformed American Culture, from Slavery to Richard Pryor.* New York: Simon & Schuster, 64.

17. William Schechter. 1970. *The History of Negro Humor in America.* New York: Fleet Press, 33.

18. W. E. B DuBois. 1961. *The Souls of Black Folk.* Greenwich, CT: Fawcett Publications, 17.

19. Richard Wright. 1937. *Black Boy: A Record of Childhood and Youth.* New York: Harper and Brothers Publishers.

20. Frederick Douglass. 1983. *The Life and Times of Frederick Douglass.* Secaucus, NJ: Citadel Press (Facsimile Edition).

21. Leslie H. Fishel and Benjamin Quarles. 1967. *The Negro American: A Documentary History.* Glenview, Il: Scott, Foresman and Company, 21.

22. Johnson and Smith, 339.

23. Ibid., 274.

24. Ibid., 106

25. Deborah White. 1999. *Ar'N't I a Woman: Female Slaves in the Plantation South.* New York: W.W. Norton, 27–61.

26. Johnson, 84 ; Johnson and Smith, 24.

27. White, 50.

28. David K. Wiggins. 1979. "Sport and Popular Pastimes in the Plantation Community: The Slave Experience" (Ph. D. diss., University of Maryland). Ann Arbor, MI: University Microfilms International, 26–27.

29. Wiggins, 17.

30. John H. Franklin and Loren Schweninger. 1999. *Runaway Slaves: Rebels on the Plantation*. New York: Oxford University Press.. This book provides explicit details on runaway slaves and their lives.

31. Ibid, 98.

32. John W. Blassingame. 1979. *The Slave Community*. New York/Oxford: Oxford University Press, 192–222.

33. Frederick Douglass. 1845/1960. *Narrative of the Life of Frederick Douglass*. Cambridge, MA: Belknap Press, 38.

34. Ibid.

35. Ibid., 183.

36. Lawrence W. Levine. 1977. *Black Culture and Black Consciousness: Afro-American Folk Thought from Slavery to Freedom*. New York: Oxford University Press, 6.

37. Blassingame, 108; Bell Wiley. 1938. *Southern Negroes: 1861–1865*. Baton Rouge: Louisiana State University Press, 24–43.

38. Johnson and Smith, 274.

39. White, 117.

40. Ibid., 100.

41. Ibid., 123.

42. George Rawick. 1972. *Arkansas Narratives* and *Missouri Narratives*, vol. 11, *The American Slave: A Composite Narrative*. Westport, CT: Greenwood Publishing Company, 145.

43. G. Johnson, 554.

44. Blassingame, 115.

45. Virginia Hamilton. 1985. *The People Could Fly: American Black Folktales*. New York: Scholastic Inc., 147–50.

46. John W. Work. 1915. Cited in C. Eric Lincoln, ed. 1974. *The Black Experience in Religion*. Garden City, NY: Anchor Books.

47. Blassingame, 37.

48. Ibid.

49. Ibid., 36.

50. Ibid., 38.

51. Harold Courlander. 1960. *The Drum and the Hoe: Life and Lore of the Haitian People*. Berkeley: University of California Press, 6.

52. Lynne Fauley Emery. 1988. *Black Dance: From 1619 to Today*, 2nd ed. Princeton, NJ: Princeton Book Company; Pere Labat. 1724. *Nouveau Voyage Aux Isles de l'Amerique*. Trans. Anthony Bliss, 2 vols. Cited in Emery, 21–22.

53. Edward Thorpe. 1990. *Black Dance*. Woodstock, NY: Overlook Press, 14.

54. Emery, 21–22.

55. De M. L. E. Moreau de St. Mery. 1796. *Danse*. Trans. Anthony Bliss, 25. Cited in Emery, 45.

56. John G. Wurdemann. 1844. *Notes on Cuba, Containing an Account of Its Discovery and Early History; a Description of the Face of the Country, Its Institutions, and the Manners and Customs of its Inhabitants, With Directions to Travelers*. Boston: James Munroe and Company, 113. Cited in Emery, 27.

57. Emery, 91–92.

58. Watkins, 143.

59. Ibid., 145.

60. Thorpe, 28.

61. Ibid., 29–30.

62. Charles Lyell. 1849. *A Second Visit to the United States of North America*, vol. 1. New York: Harper and Brothers, 269–70. Cited in Emery, 121.

63. H. G. Spaulding. 1863. Under the palmetto. *Continental Monthly* IV (July-December): 197. Cited in Emery, 123.

64. G. Johnson, 152.

65. Ibid., 551.

66. Wiggins, 37.

67. J. H. Ericson, ed. 1972. *Focus on dance VI: Ethnic and recreational dance.* Reston, VA: American Association for Health, Physical Education, and Recreational Dance, 21.

68. Wiggins, 39.

69. G. Johnson, 551.

70. Wiggins, 163.

71. G. Johnson, 552.

72. Wiggins, 293.

73. Rawick, *Arkansas Narratives*, 51–52.

74. Ibid., 69.

75. Ibid., 68.

76. Ibid., 258.

77. *See* Blassingame; *see also* Robert W. Fogel and Stanley L. Engerman. 1974. *Time on the Cross: The Economics of American Negro Slavery.* Boston: Little, Brown. These offer specific accounts of slave hunting and fishing.

78. Wiggins, 135.

79. Ibid., 144.

80. T. L. Webber. 1978. *Deep Like the Rivers: Education in the Slave Quarter Community, 1831–1865.* New York: W. W. Norton, 180–209.

81. Rawick, *Missouri Narratives*, 205–206.

82. Rawick, *Arkansas Narratives*, 21.

83. Alexander, 95–96.

84. Johnson and Smith, 132–33.

85. Rawick, *Georgia Narratives*, vols. 12–13, 260–61.

86. Webber, 215–23.

87. Rawick, *Alabama Narratives*, vol. 6, 387–88.

88. Wiggins, 56.

89. White, 92.

90. Wiggins, 57 –58.

91. Ibid.

92. For a comprehensive account of black folklore, *see* Harold Courlander. 1976. *A Treasury of Afro-American Folklore.* New York: Crown Publishers.

93. Lyle Saxon, Edward Dreyer, and Robert Tallant. 1945. *Gumbo Ya Ya: A Collection of Louisiana Folk Tales.* Boston: Houghton Mifflin, 447.

94. Webber, 183.

95. Tristram P. Coffin and Hennig Cohen, eds. 1966. *Folklore in America: Tales, Songs, Superstitions, Proverbs, Riddles, Games, Folk Drama and Folk Festivals.* Garden City, NY: Doubleday & Co., 181–82.

96. Webber, 222.

97. Wiggins, 59–60.
98. Rawick, *Arkansas Narratives*, 227.
99. Ibid., 249.
100. Webber, 186.
101. Rawick, *Arkansas Narratives*, 242.
102. Rawick, *Arkansas/Missouri Narratives*, 155.

PART TWO

Chapter 4

LIFE, RECREATION, AND LEISURE AFTER SLAVERY

How did life change in the period between slavery's end in 1865 and the historic *Brown v. Board of Education* decision in 1954, which eliminated the separate-but-equal doctrine? This period is highlighted because as newly freed Americans blacks had legitimate claims to all the rights and liberties afforded to all citizens. Yet there was an obvious gap in the basic rights, including recreation and leisure opportunities, allotted to blacks.

After slavery Americans addressed the rights of blacks by initiating the separate-but-equal doctrine. However, the country was a long way from true equality. During Reconstruction, a wide variety of factors affected blacks and their recreation and leisure: the minstrel show, radio, television, and the black church, to name a few. Both public and commercial recreation activities are discussed in terms of their impact on the black recreation experience. Ernest Attwell, one of America's pioneering black recreation leaders, is introduced and his educational and philosophical development are reviewed. Finally, important federal initiatives that fostered black involvement in American recreation and leisure are explicated.

Playing Outside of Bondage

The year was 1885, some twenty years after the end of the Civil War, and America was still adjusting to life without slaves. Many saw promise for the future of the country as it abandoned its traditional practice of holding blacks in bondage, but many whites couldn't adjust to the idea of blacks being free—and some of those whites were angry.

Ed and April "Tootie" Robinson, both black former slaves in their mid-forties lived on the outskirts of the small town of Salem, Mississippi. Most blacks in the area lived either in the most run-down part of Salem or as Ed and Tootie did on the outskirts of the town. The couple had been as excited as any black person could be when it was announced that the slaves were free. Some blacks could not internalize the reality of freedom, but those who really understood the meaning of the outcome of the War were eager to embrace their new-found fortune. They moved as quickly and as far away as possible from their former slave plantations, and those who could eventually migrated North. Those who couldn't settled wherever they found a place, most often in southern rural areas. Eventually, many blacks in the South and the North formed their owned communities in cities, separate from whites.

Ed and April, who were legally married shortly after the War, had four children: Mica, Wilfred, Sadie, and Becca. Times were difficult for Ed and his family. The only job Ed could find was as a janitor, at the local factory working long hours for menial wages. April tried to supplement the family income by babysitting and cleaning houses for local whites. Despite their scant resources, Ed and April were persistent, thrifty, and—considering their situation—good providers. Like all parents they wanted the best for their children—that is, to grow up healthy and happy with all the opportunities available to children at that time. They saved what little they could, thinking that after the War hostilities would fade and whites would allow black children to take advantage of the same opportunities afforded to white children. This was not, in fact, the case; instead, many whites were reluctant to provide equal opportunity for blacks.

Mica, Wilfred, Sadie, and Becca were healthy children who liked to play and socialize with other children. As they mastered skills in some activities, they looked to the challenges of different ones. However, as each child reached the teen years when adolescents typically expand their play interests and partners, their play opportunities were stifled. White children might travel significant distances from their homes to new or different activities, but Ed and April's children were limited to whatever recreation and leisure activities existed within their community.

America's social environment had much to do with this. The KKK was active, and black parents taught their children to stay close to the black community where there was some element of safety. If blacks traveled outside their local communities, there was no telling what they might be subjected to. Even aside from the KKK, they might run into unfriendly whites who would commit unlawful acts against blacks. In addition, people who traveled needed places to eat and places to stay.

The Limits of Black "Freedom"

"How this uneducated, socioeconomically and politically disenfranchised, habitually dependent mass of black 'citizens' managed to survive in a hostile society, and yet continue to build their economic, social and cultural base, is a wonder."[1] Ira Hutchinson, one of the few early black recreation educators and currently a member of the Roundtable Associates, wrote these words some twenty years ago while analyzing the status of blacks after emancipation. Hutchinson's assessment was accurate. How could a people so despised by the majority, so socially handicapped in the public domain, and whose African heritage had been so purposefully disdained and diffused—how could such people progress and strive in America in the period immediately after slavery?

Although the years of slavery were undoubtedly horrific, it was after slavery that some of the most serious manifestations of racism, prejudice, and hatred came to light. Many southern whites, outraged by the results of the Civil War, would not allow anything close to equality for blacks. The typical attitude of these whites made clear that, if blacks wondered how they would be treated after the War, they would be treated *exactly* as they were before the War. Such people refused to change, regardless of the outcome of the War. Indeed there was an upsurge in mistreatment of newly freed blacks. Adding to the fact that many whites had difficulty accepting the law of the land, the South was in turmoil after the Civil War, and many other issues required immediate and serious attention.

The Reconstruction Period (1865–1877) was one of the most unprecedented periods in U.S. history. The country began to rebuild in the aftermath of slavery, and initially the emerging nation offered a great deal of promise. America was grappling with many significant issues, including the question of how to treat the newly freed blacks and what rights to give these newest citizens.

The period began positively and proactively with the Civil Rights Act of 1866, giving blacks full citizenship and the promise of equal treatment under the law. American history shows that these promises were not fulfilled. Then the Reconstruction Act of 1867 was passed to ensure protection for the political rights of American blacks. These newly acquired liberties were intimidating for the newly free, but many blacks sought to meet the challenges cautiously yet positively, with a limited engagement in selected dimensions of American political life.

These liberties placed blacks in an infinitely better situation than they had enjoyed before the Civil War. They were officially free from the drudgery of slavery, they could vote, and they were entitled to hold political office. Many ex-slaves, therefore, were influential in the election of progressive lawmakers. For example, it was a well-accepted fact that the black vote was particularly instrumental in the creation and development of schools for black children. Many of these ideas were the brainchildren of forward-thinking white lawmakers.

The Reconstruction period, with all its promise, still did not offer blacks the reality of full citizenship. The period was marked by lack of opportunity and by unlawful discrimination against blacks in virtually all aspects of American life. Many of the liberties promised during Reconstruction were phantom promises made of words and not of realities. Blacks were still effectively denied adequate housing and employment, and this discrimination spilled over into the play, recreation, and leisure activities and opportunities of blacks.

After the Civil War, America broadened its recreation interests. The 1880s and 1890s were marked by an expansion of recreation and leisure which continued through the Industrial Revolution and into the early part of the twentieth century. Prior to this time, there were really no formally organized recreational activities or sports in America. This expansion was brought on partly by the incremental urbanization of the nation.

With this urbanization most Americans, except for blacks, crossed new frontiers of recreational involvement. The once typical activities like fishing and hunting gave way to more organized and sophisticated group or "collegiate" recreations and to sports like polo, bicycling, and track and field.

Although the puritan ethic was still predominant and America was still very influenced by the dollar, Americans began to realize a societal need for more play, recreation, and leisure. Engagement in these pursuits was thought to add to the overall quality of life. This growth in recreational involvement was first evident in commercial recreation[2] where consumers pay directly for services rendered. Urban commercial recreation for youth grew at an accelerated rate in the early part of the century as families paid for their children to engage in various forms of recreation. However, the increase in commercial recreation, which at the time encompassed many activities involving large groups, shifted attention to recreation from children to adults. Consequently, adults devoted more time and money to recreation and leisure in ways that had been unheard of. This ideological transition took place primarily in urban areas because recreation in rural areas was slower-paced.

This philosophical change was manifested in the work life of Americans. Supported by the Playground Association of America (PAA), legislation gradually decreased the traditional twelve-hour workday to the ten-hour workday and eventually to the eight-hour workday.[3] Americans began to accept such innovations as Saturday half-holidays and two-week vacations. Eventually, these became widely accepted and then expected.

The media had a definitive impact on the acceptance of additional time for recreation and leisure. The news media devoted significant coverage to sports, recreation, and leisure. Newspapers and magazines increased the numbers of columns addressing recreation and leisure pursuits. At the same time, outdoor recreation activities experienced a decisive growth in momentum and participation. Activities such as walking, mountain climbing, fishing, hunting, canoeing, and camping were in vogue for many Americans.[4]

The radical idea of *vacationing* gained popularity. Newspapers began to advertise resort facilities. Foster Dulles, one of the early recreation historians, reported that in May 1890 the *New York Tribune* ran eight columns solely for the marketing of vacation facilities, something unheard of in prior years. These had previously been activities reserved for the wealthy. What was so unusual was that these advertisements were aimed at middle-class Americans. The most obvious attraction for the middle class was moderately priced hotels and travel. Such pricing made it possible for the more average American to enjoy a broader range of recreation and leisure pursuits.

White Recreation in the Reconstruction and Industrial Periods

For many scholars the period from about 1900 through the 1920s marked the beginning of modern American society, recording amazing growth in many areas, including recreation. As citizens of a developing nation, Americans became aware of the intrinsic values and benefits of recreation. The colonial and aristocratic attitudes that recreation and leisure pursuits were only for the wealthy were rapidly dissipating, and more cities were providing organized recreation for their citizens. Community recreation centers, a new phenomenon, began offering more varied programming, and the national park system set aside large amounts of land specifically for recreational use. All facets of recreation increased during the 1920s. With the enactment of the eight-hour workday, Americans sought expanded public recreation for their free-time.[5]

More than ever, whites began to broaden the range of their

recreation and leisure pleasures.[6] The most dramatic increase appeared in the lives of urban white Americans, but this was repulsive to many rural whites. To them, the larger cities represented corruption and wickedness. They resisted such temptations and sought to maintain the status quo in rural America.

For many rural southern whites, then, recreation and leisure remained in the traditional mode. Southern life and recreation were slower-paced. Recreation and leisure could be enjoyed just about everywhere, including such typical activities as lounging around the house or sitting and talking on porches in the afternoons and evenings as the searing summer heat gradually diminished.

The aristocratic South had a reputation as the most religiously relaxed region in the United States. The puritan work ethic was incrementally dissipating, so there were few strict rules concerning recreation and leisure. Consequently, southern whites were free to entertain themselves without worrying about "wasting time."

After slavery, the most popular recreation activities for poorer whites were hunting and fishing, along with occasional farm festivals in the form of corn-shuckings, log-rollings, and cotton-pickings. Occasionally they attended horse races or cock fights, and sometimes a circus or some other traveling entertainment added excitement.[7] While the wealthy engaged in formal balls, fashionable picnics, and chivalric tournaments, these entertainments were generally unavailable to the majority of the population. Wealthier whites also engaged in lawn tennis, croquet, roller skating, and archery after slavery.[8]

In contrast to the South, the North (particularly due to urbanization during the Industrial Revolution) offered a broader range of additional recreation outlets, including the theater, minstrel shows, circuses, amusement parks, public dance facilities, and horse racing.[9] Whites residing in urban areas were offered a broad range of activities.

Black Recreation in the Reconstruction and Industrial Periods

After slavery, throughout the Reconstruction and industrial periods, the geographic population distribution of blacks significantly changed. In 1900 nearly 90 percent of blacks lived in the South. Approximately one-quarter of this number were classified as urban residents.[10] A significant migration of rural Southern blacks to urban areas in the South and North took place in the late nineteenth and early twentieth centuries. It was estimated that from 1916 to 1918 approximately five hundred thousand blacks moved to northern cities.[11] The black population of Chicago increased from 30,150 in 1900 to 233,903 in 1930. In New York the black population also recorded significant growth—from 60,666 to 327,706 between 1920 and 1930.[12] Significantly, the perception that urban areas offered more recreation opportunities was identified as one contributing reason for the migration. Early scholar George Haynes wrote, "Negroes believe that the Negro community in the North, although considerably segregated, has advantages over the former homes in the South, such as theatres, public libraries, parks, playgrounds, museums, and no 'Jim Crow' railroad and street cars."[13]

Meanwhile, whites—especially those residing in the South—were particularly unconcerned about blacks' recreation and leisure. Southern whites wanted little to do with blacks. For the most part, as long as blacks and their recreation could be kept separate, the white majority was satisfied. They simply did not want to be closely involved with blacks in any major aspect of life, including their play, recreation, or leisure. This attitude would have an important impact on the recreation and leisure of blacks.

A number of other factors also affected the recreational, educational, and emotional well-being of newly freed blacks after slavery. Some of these prominent factors included a large exodus from the South, a lack of job opportunities, the enactment of black codes, and the growth and activity of the Ku Klux Klan. Each of these would prove detrimental in the long run to the availability and opportunity of recreation for blacks.

After the War, many blacks were eager to leave the South. Even though some were asked to stay (for whatever reasons) by their former owners, most wanted to escape the stigma of bondage by exiting the site of their enslavement. Slavery had severely limited opportunity and mobility for blacks, and now that they were free, many were determined to compensate for their long history of confinement. Those who had the resources left the South, seeking distance from the sights, locations, and connections related to their long captivity.

Others were forced to leave. Former slave owners, angry at losing the War, did not want to associate with free blacks. Most migrating blacks chose their destinations with care. Many sought out loved ones in the hope of restoring broken families and sharing the joys of their new freedom. While some free blacks, like whites, searched for new opportunities in the West, most looked to relocate to urban areas in the South and North.

Some blacks did leave the South, but many more were not as fortunate and had to remain. These formed their own communities, but there was often not much solace in the opportunity available in black communities. Black codes and the Ku Klux Klan impeded community life for newly freed blacks in the South and even for some in the North.

Black codes, later known as Jim Crow laws, were enacted in most southern states after the Civil War. These codes varied in strictness from state to state, but were all specifically aimed at restricting blacks and their movements.[14] Some truly good-natured whites believed the codes were good because they protected blacks from many of the new immoralities that would arise as a result of abrupt freedom.[15] In reality, the codes hindered equality by segregating blacks and limiting their rights to vote and to seek protection under the law, especially when whites were involved. These codes dictated, among other things, where blacks could live and work, and in some instances, when and if they could leave certain areas without the written consent of white authorities.[16] For newly freed blacks, the enforcement of these codes proved devastating to any recreation and leisure opportunity.

In addition to the initiation of black codes, the rise of the Ku Klux Klan proved a formidable obstacle to freedom for blacks. The Ku Klux Klan began with six former Confederate soldiers in Pulaski, Tennessee, in 1866. The Klan was a secret society or club whose primary mission was to maintain white supremacy. This goal appealed to many whites after the Civil War, so the Klan eventually spread to all the former Confederate states. The Klan transformed itself into a terrorist group, dedicated to keeping blacks and other non-whites in their subordinate place. Through a campaign of murder, whippings, burnings, bombings, and intimidation, the Klan created devastation throughout the South, eventually spreading to the North and West. The Klan made it difficult for blacks to feel free. Through intimidation and fear, blacks were forced to remain close to home. Thus, the fear and intimidation by the Klan negatively impacted black participation in America's broad range of recreation and leisure pursuits.

Black recreation and leisure after slavery was also influenced by a number of other prominent factors. After slavery blacks were separated in society and were not allowed adequate use of public or private recreation facilities.[17] The few recreation facilities that blacks *were* allowed to use were not adequately supplied with materials or professionally trained management. Second, the geographical location most blacks, particularly those residing in the rural South, meant that their recreation patterns followed those of rural Southern whites, which were generally limited. Third, because most recreation for blacks was carried out in black communities, it developed traits of its own, sometimes different from recreation in the white community.[18]

In short, whatever recreation and leisure activity a black person could engage in had to be undertaken in close proximity to the home community, which gave it certain distinguishing features. These features can be thought of as the ingredients that make "black recreation" culturally specific. The enjoyment and proficiency with which some blacks engage in such activities as, for example, basketball may be attributed to this phenomenon.

As blacks were more or less forced to engage in a limited range of activities, the extra time allotted to these recreations enhanced and developed black proficiency. This practice accords with what many parents teach: that "the more one engages in and practices something, the more proficient he or she will become in that activity." However, the simplicity of this parental teaching may not always be applicable to a cultural transition. Cultural transitioning, defined as what is passed on from one generation to another, may take generations to incorporate new skills, attitudes, and behaviors. The history of neglect of black recreation, then, suggests that the recreation and leisure interests and development of blacks might naturally lag behind that of whites in some recreation and leisure pursuits.

During slavery, it was common for whites to make fun of and criticize blacks. After the Civil War and into the early part of the twentieth century, continuous and often intense criticism of blacks persisted. Even what blacks did in their limited recreation and leisure drew criticism and subjective evaluation from whites. Whites were free to engage in virtually unlimited recreation and leisure pursuits, and they were also quick to judge the less fortunate blacks and their recreation. Clinging to the mindset of many whites during slavery—the belief that blacks did not have high levels of human capabilities—whites thought that recreation and leisure for blacks was primarily a means of filling dull and empty days or simply relief from long, hard, monotonous labor. In this respect some whites described black recreation as purposeless. They failed to see the essence of black recreation and leisure engagement. These whites could not conceive that blacks knew how to engage "properly" in recreation and leisure.

Consequently, stereotypical myths of black recreation were born. Whites' ideas of black recreation and leisure were largely inadequate and based on incorrect data. For example, many whites believed through their limited observations that blacks spent most of their free time loafing, boasting, telling exaggerated stories, singing, and dancing. In reality, many blacks did "take it easy" during their free time. Indeed, logically blacks would seek the rest and relaxation of which they had been deprived. But white criticism that blacks loafed and were naturally lazy was irrational and illogical. Whites had traveled across the ocean through numerous dangers including raging storms, excessive heat, and unbearable cold, in order to bring blacks to America. Why would they travel such a distance through such perils to bring back lazy people? In fact, blacks were good workers, capable and productive. Subconsciously, whites must have known this.

Another stereotypical myth attributed to blacks an excessive aggressiveness. Nothing could be further from the truth, but, of course, when engaging in some of the more physical forms of recreation, blacks could appear aggressive. To many whites, such aggression was viewed as barbaric and irrational, yet these same whites did not view the inhumane treatment of slaves as barbaric.

In some ways blacks set a tone for the level of intensity in some of today's recreations and sports such as basketball and football, an intensity which is now emulated by many Americans. As whites observed blacks engaging in some activities, they characterized their behavior as hostile, rude, or harsh. To white observers, blacks might appear combative, contentious, and even out of control. Whites unfamiliar with black culture viewed black recreation as aggressive and obscene. Many whites contended that black recreational behavior was unrestrained and uninhibited and certainly not constructive in terms of physical or mental skill development.

Consequently, multiple societal factors came into play, each with an impact on black recreation. Unlike slaves, emancipated blacks were "free" to pursue and participate in leisure and recreational activities. Economic deprivation limited blacks to a narrow range of recreational pursuits. Typical games and activities included baseball, marbles, card-playing, swimming, dancing, and church entertainments. For those few who could afford it, going to movies, attending local fairs and traveling minstrel shows, hunting, fishing, and visiting with others provided additional recreational opportunities.[19]

Many of these opportunities and activities had previously been closed to blacks. If and when they were allowed access to these activities after slavery, they were usually restricted to separate seating and separate participation times. Yet, these group opportunities were the popular activities of the day.

Notes/References

1. Ira Hutchinson. 1983. "Recreation and Racial Minorities." In *Recreation and Special Populations*, 2nd ed. Boston: Allyn and Bacon, 342.

2. Benjamin K. Hunnicutt. 1988. *Work Without End: Abandoning Short Hours for the Right to Work*. Philadelphia, PA: Temple University Press, 110.

3. Hunnicutt, 1.

4. Foster Dulles. 1965. *A History of Recreation: America Learns to Play*, 2nd ed. New York: Meredith Publishing Company, 202.

5. Hunnicutt, 110–11.

6. John S. Ezell. 1975. *The South Since 1865*, 2nd ed. New York: Macmillan Publishing, 322.

7. Dulles, 22–66.

8. Ibid., 182.

9. Ibid., 354.

10. J. J. Pilz. 1985. "The Beginnings of Organized Play for Black Americans: E.T. Attwell and the PRAA." *Journal of Negro History* 70, no. 3/4 (Summer-Autumn): 59–72.

11. August Meier and Elliott Rudwick. 1966. *From Plantation to Ghetto: An Interpretive History of American Negroes*. New York: Hill and Wang Publishers, 189–92.

12. Richard B. Sherman, ed. 1970. *The Negro and the City*. Englewood Cliffs, NJ: Prentice-Hall, 5.

13. George Haynes. 1934. Negro migration—Its effect on family and community life in the North," *National Conference on Social Work* 51 (71).

14. Leslie H. Fishel and Benjamin Quarles. 1967. *The Negro American: A Documentary History*. Glenview, IL: Scott, Foresman and Company, 21–26.

15. Mel Watkins. 1994. *On the Real Side: Laughing, Lying, and Signifying— The Underground Tradition of African-American Humor That Transformed American Culture, from Slavery to Richard Pryor*. New York: Simon & Schuster, 122.

16. William Julius Wilson. 1966. *The Declining Significance of Race: Blacks and Changing American Institutions,* 2nd ed. Chicago: University of Chicago Press, 53.

17. Ezell, 184–87.

18. Gunnar Myrdal. 1944. *An American Dilemma: The Negro Problem and Modern Democracy*. New York: Harper and Brothers Publishers, 982.

19. Watkins, 80–133; Arthur F. Raper. 1936. *Preface to Peasantry: A Tale of Two Black Belt Counties*. Chapel Hill: University of North Carolina Press, 387–403.

Chapter Five

ENTERTAINMENT AFTER SLAVERY

The Minstrel Show

Minstrel shows—traveling entertainment consisting of skits, songs, and dances—were initially developed for the entertainment of white audiences. Although they originated as early as the 1820s, minstrel shows grew in popularity up to and after emancipation. They usually involved a conglomeration of plays, dances, songs, jugglers, acrobats, and trained animals along with black-faced actors who mimicked and mocked blacks. The black-faced acts were particularly amusing to white audiences who saw blackness as something to be laughed at.

After slavery the minstrel show continued to be popular. These shows were a prime means of perpetuating supposedly humorous negative black stereotypes.[1] As the shows became a preeminent form of entertainment, they etched a distorted image of blacks in the minds of white audiences. Eventually, the shows evolved into a systematized form of black-faced entertainment, with white males playing the roles of black characters.

The shows were more than entertainment for whites; they also displayed and reaffirmed whites' attitudes about blacks. Before the 1850s, most white Americans had been content to accept the notion that slaves were happy, basking in southern hospitality and wanting nothing more than to continue their jolly lives, free from the responsibilities that encumbered whites. The minstrel show reinforced this view.

Seldom if ever were theatrical portrayals of blacks sympathetic. Most often blacks were shown as incompetent, untrustworthy, and ignorant, and these themes dominated the content of the minstrel show. William Schechter, in *The History of Negro Humor in America*, described a typically demeaning joke:

> "Say Pomp, you nigger, where did you get that new hat?"
> "Why, at de shop, ob course."
> "What is de price of such a hat as dat?"
> "I don't know, nigger, I don't know—de shopkeeper wasn't dar!"[2]

Initially, blacks did not perform in minstrel shows. Although slaves had frequently entertained their masters (often for the slave owners' profit), few had received any extended notoriety for their talents. However, blacks were used as minstrel performers as early as the 1840s, and an all-black company was formed in the early 1860s. Not until after slavery did a black person take on the entrepreneurial role. Immediately after slavery ended, a black performer named Charles "Barney" Hicks organized the first permanent black minstrel company in Indianapolis, Indiana—the Georgia Minstrels. Hicks faced numerous difficulties in dealing with white theater managers and was eventually forced to sell his rights to the company to a white man named Charles Callender.[3]

After slavery, more black men and women began to appear in minstrel shows. In 1891 the first black woman, Dora Dean, was cast in *The Creole Show*, a minstrel show in New York, to perform the famous cakewalk dance.[4] Interestingly—though demoralizingly—minstrelsy provided one of the first vehicles through which a limited number of blacks could make a living outside farming. One of the most significant features of black minstrelsy was its provision of a mechanism for the development of America's black musical and comedy professionals.

Although some blacks, particularly the more educated, resented black minstrel performers portraying blacks as inept, many used the minstrel show for their own entertainment and employment.

Minstrel shows were, as noted above, intended as entertainment for white-only audiences. However, the addition and popularity of black minstrel performers brought many blacks to see these performances as well. Billy Kersands was one of most sought-after black minstrel performers. Kersands' name on a town's billboard could fill the whole town with excitement. Whites and blacks lined up to attend his shows, partly for the sheer entertainment they provided and partly to see a famous individual "in person." Even though blacks were mocked in much of the minstrel show's content, it was inspirational for black audiences to see a person of their race actually become famous. When minstrel shows came to town, theater owners occasionally allowed blacks to attend by roping off a small section of the gallery or balcony (referred to as "Nigger Heaven").[5] This allowance was made to increase revenue, not to include blacks in an equal democratic society.

As minstrel shows gained popularity, blacks began their own minstrel troupes and comprised the majority of the audience for these black-only troupes, whose appearances became notable entertainment events in the black community.

Radio and American Recreation

Electronic technology introduced in the early part of the century also had an important impact on the recreation and leisure patterns of Americans. November 2, 1920, marked one of the most important of these technological advances. On that day commercially licensed radio was introduced in the United States. Although radio's initial impact was minimal due to its low budgets and immature technology, it gradually altered Americans' use of free time. The popularity of radio was phenomenal both as a business and as entertainment. As a business, by the end of 1922—less than two years from its beginning—there were 576 licensed stations, and radio sales increased from one million in 1920 to four million in 1925.[6] This gave radio a formidable influence on American life because many people began to devote considerable free time to listening to the radio.

Most early programming consisted of news, the music of local musicians, commentaries on such live events as boxing matches or concerts, and live comic monologues. Americans were delighted to hear of events *as they occurred*. Radio was a phenomenal technological achievement. The new medium required Americans to use their imaginations and creativity. Live broadcasts allowed people relaxing at home to receive a broad-based array of information. Additionally, radio allowed individuals who could not afford more expensive commercial entertainments greater options for their free time. Indeed, radio was the nation's most popular form of entertainment and most significant cultural medium during the early part of the twentieth century.

As a relatively inexpensive outlet, radio was readily accessible to most white Americans. For blacks, radio followed the traditional course established by all aspects of mainstream American life: they were the last to have access to the medium, and it offered virtually no acknowledgment of African Americans. Significant events in the black community, such as the Harlem Renaissance and the continued struggle for equal opportunity, were seldom addressed on the radio. However, a few very gifted blacks were allowed to participate as guests of noted white musicians. Not until the civil unrest of the 1960s did radio give serious attention to African Americans and their communities.

As a result of this lack of participation by African Americans on the radio, the black audience was initially small. Blacks began to listen more earnestly as radio programming offered more air time to African Americans in the entertainment industry. Initially, the attention given to blacks on the radio followed the pattern established by the minstrel show in which black-faced white actors played the roles of blacks. This role-play has been identified as "racial ventriloquy." In the beginning, when programs were not broadcast before live audiences, the black audience was larger. Many black listeners may have believed that performers on the radio were black. This ventriloquy was instrumental in establishing stereotyped images of African Americans that lasted for decades.

When blacks were finally allowed in radio, they were successful. One of the most popular early radio programs was *Amos and Andy*, probably the first nationally successful black-dialect radio program. Initially the black characters were played by white performers, but *Amos and Andy*, like the minstrel show, gained more popularity (especially in the black community) when it included black performers.[7] The program seemed to have created a national obsession during its peak years.

Radio became a major form of free-time entertainment for blacks and whites, perhaps especially for blacks because the Klan was very active and blacks were limited in where they could safely go. By 1935 approximately 70 percent of U.S. homes had radios, and some forty million Americans tuned in each night.[8] Clearly, the basic structure of recreation and leisure in America would be significantly altered by the technological success of radio.

Notes/References

1. Mel Watkins. 1994. *On the Real Side: Laughing, Lying, and Signifying—The Underground Tradition of African-American Humor That Transformed American Culture, from Slavery to Richard Pryor.* New York: Simon & Schuster, 82.

2. William Schechter. 1970. *The History of Negro Humor in America.* New York: Fleet Press, 56–57.

3. Jessie Carney Smith, ed. 1994. *Black Firsts: 2,000 Years of Extraordinary Achievement.* Detroit, MI: Visible Ink Press, 43.

4. Ibid.

5. Watkins, 125.

6. Watkins, 267.

7. Watkins, 267–324.

8. Watkins, 268.

Chapter Six

SEPARATE AND UNEQUAL

Philosophically, one of the major purposes of the organized public recreation enterprise has been to provide quality services, facilities, and leadership to *all* of America's citizens. Public services initially occupied a significant strategic impact on race relations, especially in the South, because as municipal facilities assumed broader responsibility, blacks could begin to lay claim to services previously reserved only for whites. Nonetheless, even with the inclusion of more municipal recreation, equalization of public services was not achievable for blacks. Black and white public services in municipal recreation were "separate and unequal."

Segregation and Discrimination in America

The beginning of legalized separation in America started on June 7, 1892, when Homer Plessy, a thirty-year-old mixed-race shoemaker was jailed for sitting in the "white" train car of the East

Louisiana Railroad. Plessy was only part black (one-eighth black and seven-eighths white), but under a Louisiana act mandating separate train cars for blacks and whites, he was considered black and required to sit in the car designated for blacks and "colored" persons. Plessy took his case to local court and argued that the "separate car law" violated the Thirteenth and Fourteenth Amendments to the Constitution. He lost at every level, and lawful separateness of facilities continued.

Yet significantly, the Supreme Court maintained that facilities for blacks and for whites should be *equal*. The *Plessy v. Ferguson* decision marked the beginning of legal segregation in America and allowed states to establish racially segregated facilities as long as the accommodations and facilities in public institutions were equal. The separate-but-equal doctrine was quickly extended to cover many areas of public life, including restaurants, theaters, restrooms, drinking fountains, and public schools.

The *Plessy* decision upheld segregation for more than half a century and reaffirmed the constitutionality of separate-but-equal in virtually all aspects of American life, including recreation. Although the Fourteenth Amendment guaranteed all citizens equal protection under the law, in reality there was no equality in America. During the period when America was legally a separatist society, the opportunities afforded to its black citizens were minimal.

Blacks and Recreation under Separate-but-Equal

Due to such early discriminatory practices, some intentional and some not, blacks were not afforded equal opportunity. Civil rights legislation at both the federal and state levels influenced the practices of the recreation profession. The procurement and enactment of some of the most basic civil rights through the efforts of the most prominent organized recreation organizations—such as the Playground and Recreation Association of America (PRAA)—were very slow to come.

It is important to review former patterns of segregation in recreation enterprises (including recreation centers, playgrounds, swimming pools, and camps) to better understand the situation in the early part of the century. The earliest data reported regarding segregation in recreation facilities appears in the 1920s.

In the early part of the century, the "recreation center," the center of community recreation activity, was a relatively new concept. In 1927 there were 103 indoor recreation centers nationwide for blacks, only 24 of which were open year-round. In the same year only 9 new indoor recreation centers were set aside for blacks in 9 cities. Activities in the newly developed "indoor recreation center" were popular attractions in many communities. The activities included music, athletics, social recreation, dramatics, games, handicrafts, and literary and civic group functions.[1]

More specifically, public recreation was segregated and there was a general lack of facilities for blacks. The 1920s saw continued interest and growth in public recreation. The number of municipal public playgrounds increased more than 74 percent during the 1920s.[2] Virtually all these facilities were segregated. It didn't seem to matter whether the facility was located in the North or the South, segregation led to unequal opportunity and discrimination. In 1927 one of the first studies addressed black recreation participation in 57 American cities, forty northern cities and seventeen southern cities. Forrest Washington of the Atlanta School of Social Work found only "whites-only"—that is, completely segregated—facilities in investigating southern recreation facilities that included playgrounds, parks, recreation centers, bathing beaches, and swimming pools. In the North segregation was the law, but selected facilities reported no or limited segregation in many of these same enterprises.

Washington's study used the following southern cities to collect the data:

Atlanta, GA	Lexington, KY	Orlando, FL
Baltimore, MD	Macon, GA	Savannah, GA
Birmingham, AL	Memphis, TN	Richmond, VA
Columbus, GA	New Orleans, LA	Tampa, FL
Houston, TX	Norfolk, VA	Washington, DC
Jacksonville, FL	Nashville, TN	

The following northern cities were used in the study:

Atlantic City, NJ	St. Joseph, MO	Philadelphia, PA
Berkeley, CA	Kansas City, MO	Pittsburgh, PA
Burlington, IA	Lansing, MI	Rock Island, IL
Buffalo, NY	Milwaukee, WI	South Bend, IN

Canton, OH	Montclair, NJ	Sandusky, IL
Colorado Springs, CO	Minneapolis, MN	Springfield, MA
Cincinnati, OH	Morristown, NJ	St. Louis, MO
Cleveland, OH	Mason City, IA	Scranton PA
Decatur, IL	New Bedford, MA	Toledo, OH
Detroit, MI	Newark, NJ	Van Wert, OH
Duluth, MN	New York, NY	Wichita, KS
Des Moines, IA	Oakland, CA	Watertown, NY
Fort Wayne, ID	Port Huron, MI	Zanesville, OH
Indianapolis, IN		

Importantly, the southern and northern cities in Washington's study included some of the nation's largest in the 1920s. Generally in larger cities, as might be expected, people tended to be more tolerant and to interact more with other races. In essence, Washington's data points out the best that the nation had to offer at the time. This helps identify some of the realities of segregation in recreation between the end of the Civil War and 1927. However, segregation carried with it a number of consequences. It limited contact between blacks and whites, and that limited contact would eventually lead to discriminatory practices.

In fact, many blacks and whites *desired* to play together, but they had to do so in secret and in moderation. Recreational baseball was a typical example. After slavery, baseball was a popular recreational activity, especially in the South where many cities had baseball teams. Some white teams and leagues were organized with the help of local sponsors, but for the most part black baseball games consisted primarily of locals randomly organizing pick-up teams. There were few if any organized leagues for blacks. In rare instances, organized black baseball teams were formed. For example, in 1867 the Brooklyn Uniclues hosted the Philadelphia Excelsiors in a game billed as the championship of colored clubs.[3] Organized games of this type were rare, and information about them was purposely not widely distributed.

Interested blacks played the game whenever and wherever they could. While whites had access to relatively well-kept baseball fields and equipment, blacks most often played in open fields, getting by with whatever suitable equipment they could find. Eventually, many black baseball players, primarily in the Negro leagues, began to gain notoriety in black communities for their skills. When the news of their skills spread to white communities, some whites became interested in playing against these talented athletes.

While the tensions left from slavery were still relatively new, whites and blacks rarely competed in publicized contests. Generally, white teams played other white teams and blacks played among themselves; seldom did they play on the same fields or use the same equipment. Not until 1869, some four years after slavery, did a black team from Pennsylvania, the Philadelphia Pythons, play an all-white baseball team. This limited contact between blacks and whites in baseball carried over into most other areas of life.

Such limited contact was encouraged in both work and living environments. During the separate-but-equal period blacks received the least desirable part of the separation. The consequences of separation carried over into other recreation opportunities, programming, leadership, and facilities. As E.B. Henderson put it in 1940:

> Negro youth under the best of mixed-programs suffers in varying degrees in the limitations of participating opportunities because of the lack of neighborhood facilities or because of the costliness of duplication of facilities for the two groups. Frequently swimming, golf, tennis, and many other art forms are denied to Negroes in communities for one reason or another. . . For no matter how adequately equal provisions are planned, segregation almost necessarily connotes discrimination in facilities, leadership, and money expenditures. It is true for recreation as it is true for segregated systems of education.[4]

Black Participation at "White" Facilities

Slowly, as America continued to make advancements in equalizing opportunity between blacks and whites, public recreation agencies began to feel pressure to become more accommodating. However, there was little guidance at the national level to help with local problem solving. Virtually every local recreation organization determined its own solutions to the most controversial issues of the period: segregation and integration. More and more, as America incrementally became an enlightened nation, it was apparent that the days of second-class citizenship were slowly ending. Yet each organization had to use its leadership's courage, faith, beliefs, and morals as guides in this critical area of American life.

Most public recreation organizations were very cautious as they dealt with questions of program integration. In 1949 C. H. Klippel, an employee at a YMCA in Columbus, Ohio, provided the following scrupulous suggestions for professionals and agencies considering integration of camp facilities:

- Go about it quietly. Make no public announcement. Prejudice feeds on publicity.
- Make no mention in the camp literature of the change in policy. Let it evolve unostentatiously among those who wish to cooperate.
- Be sure that all parents of all races understand the nature of the camp period at the time they register for camp, so that integrated grouping does not surprise or disturb anyone when he arrives at camp.
- Strive to make the experiment successful from the beginning by making it a good demonstration of quality camping. So far as possible, especially in the first year, select campers who will cooperate in the integrated plan and eliminate those of all races whose known prejudices would make them unfit for citizenship in such a camp.
- Be sure that all counselors are free as possible from prejudice, and qualified to serve in an inter-racial setting.
- In all camp organization, relationships and programs, forget completely that there is such a thing as color or race. Never "drag" it unnaturally into a discussion nor let it influence anything that is done in camp. Recognize individual differences by giving no special consideration or favor to anyone because of race. Be color blind.[5]

The suggestions provided by Klippel reveal a definite cautionary attitude necessary for those brave enough to experiment with camp integration. Obviously, the impact of such a risky endeavor was thought to be based in part on the likely success of the experience. However, success as described by Klippel had to be ensured by highly scripted processes ranging from keeping a very low public profile to carefully choosing program participants. An interesting dichotomy in Klippel's recommendations appears in his comments on color blindness. His final comments suggest color blindness on the part of program staff, while in the early part of the analysis he recommends carefully selecting black and white program participants. In hindsight, Klippel's advice was probably wise since parts of America were only beginning to experiment with integration. The advice was to proceed cautiously if you were going to proceed at all.

Public Recreation

Initially, the public recreation profession, like most other public service professions, was influenced by the commonly accepted patterns of segregation and discrimination, and consequently did not adequately fulfill its obligation to provide equal services to blacks. During the separate-but-equal period, public recreation had many acknowledged aims and objectives. Some were particular to racial-group understanding and included the following:

1. To break down race, class, and religious prejudice
2. To reduce juvenile delinquency and reduce crime
3. To educate for character through plays and games
4. To develop community spirit and civic pride by bringing neighbors together in play
5. To promote, control, and regulate proper leisure time activities.

Yet while the separate-but-equal philosophy prevailed, some whites believed that blacks—particularly black youth—could prosper through well-trained leadership.[6]

Again, elaborate and precise statistical information relating to blacks and public recreational programming and facility usage between slavery and the mid-twentieth century is sparse. However, the available data provides some revealing information about black access to public recreation and black recreation opportunity in general.

After slavery large numbers of blacks migrated to the North. Most of these individuals settled in industrial cities. The reasons

for the migration were numerous: poor housing and neighborhood conditions in the South; poor schools for black children;
lack of justice in southern courts; and dreams of greater freedom,
independence, and opportunity. Although life in the North offered
more opportunity, it also presented many problems. Problems
arose at parks and playgrounds, in facility usage, in leadership, and
in land acquisition.

Parks and Playgrounds

C. H. Klippel's recommendations for integration were directed at
camp settings. Camps were uniquely situated "out of the public
eye." Black participation in white parks and playgrounds was a
different matter altogether. Most whites simply did not want
blacks in "their" parks and playgrounds, using "their" equipment, or playing with their children. As a result, black use of public parks and playgrounds was very limited. Even when blacks
were allowed to use some public parks designated for whites,
which was uncommon especially in the South, their activity was
restricted. In many designated "white parks," blacks might be
allowed only to sit, walk through, and enjoy some of the park's
sights and sounds but not to use the playgrounds.[7] In some
southern cities—for example Richmond, Virginia—black use of
public parks was restricted to walking, sitting, and possibly fishing.[8] At the same time, whites were free to use the parks to their
fullest potential, denied access to none of the facilities.

In most early community planning, recreation opportunity for
blacks, even for black youth, was not realistically addressed,
though black youths were clearly much in need. Recreation for
blacks was virtually ignored or at best only modestly considered.
The 1920s marked a new era, beginning some serious, although
limited, examinations of the leisure-related behaviors of African
Americans. Early testimony points to inadequacies in public recreation that may have been contributing factors to the problem of
black adolescents and adults seeking illegitimate recreation activity. Several other early reports indicated that lack of public recreational facilities was a contributing factor to high crime among
both juveniles and adults.[9]

Similarly, in 1927 the National Urban League of Fort Wayne,

Indiana, conducted a survey of blacks in the city. This was one of the most significant studies of the time, notable because its results indicated that[10] when adequate recreation was provided in playgrounds, it was most often provided only for the youngest children, leaving older black children with relatively unattractive recreation options.[11] This lack of public recreation opportunity, although initially difficult to verify empirically, could prove significant for blacks, black communities, and black quality of life, implying a potential reduction in black juvenile-related crime activity.

In Washington, D.C., a 1927 study by William H. Jones, a professor from Howard University, revealed that there were twenty-five playgrounds for blacks, but only one with a swimming pool. Professor Jones concluded that inadequate recreation for blacks contributed to problems of community disorganization, prostitution, gambling, alcoholism, and hidden nightlife.[12]

Then in 1928 in Fort Wayne, Indiana, Professor Jones conducted another study which concluded that inadequacies in black recreation facilities offered through public recreation organizations was one reason why many blacks sought illegitimate recreation. Charles Johnson, a scholar from Fisk University, was another black researcher who brought to light the plight of blacks as part of his comprehensive research in the 1920s. Johnson analyzed statistical data from the seventy-five cities with the largest black populations and found that even in the North parks and playgrounds for blacks were inadequate. Where long-established black communities were located close to city parks, most were freely open to blacks; yet many of these were mismanaged and tended to have inferior equipment. In the North, although blacks had access to most parks, frequent racial friction negatively influenced black attendance. Johnson observed that in some northern and border cities, playgrounds located near black communities, even those with both white and black leadership, were attended by only a small fraction of the black children of playground age.[13] Based on Johnson's work, three very influential determinants of the quality of black recreation in the 1920s were pinpointed: inferior equipment, potential racial confrontation with whites, and lack of trained leaders.

Johnson's research findings on southern recreation were also revealing. In the South, recreational space and equipment for blacks were also very inadequate. Unless specifically set aside for blacks, public recreation facilities were assumed to be for the exclusive use of whites.

In the early 1900s as they emerged from centuries of oppression in America, blacks were probably more in need of structured and organized recreation than whites. Yet blacks had inferior recreational programming, leadership, and facilities. For example, a significant proportion of play materials for black children in black communities were not provided through public funding, and it was difficult for black children to share the play equipment provided by urban municipalities for white children. Gunnar Myrdal addressed this situation in his classic book *An American Dilemma: The Negro Problem and Democracy*, writing, "The visitor finds everywhere in the South that not only beaches and playgrounds, but also public parks are often entirely closed to Negroes, except for Negro nurses watching white children."[14]

Many of America's largest cities, even those in the North and West where the arm of racial prejudice and discrimination was supposedly not as far-reaching, offered inequitable public recreation facilities and options. In 1920 Cleveland, Ohio, had 81 playgrounds, of which blacks could use only 8. In the same year Denver, Colorado, had a population of 212,024 whites and 6,705 blacks, but African Americans were allowed to use only 2 of the city's playgrounds. In Philadelphia, Pennsylvania, while the 1920 census indicated a population of 1,290,253 whites and 134,229 blacks, there were 90 board-of-education-administered playgrounds; however, blacks were allowed use of only 24. Further, Johnson observed that for the most part in the North schoolyards had to suffice as playgrounds for blacks who wanted space for recreation.[15]

In 1927 Ernest Attwell, the influential early black leader of the Playground and Recreation Association of America (PRAA) (who will be discussed in more detail later), supplied the following information about outdoor playground facilities for blacks in America: only 82 playgrounds were open year-round in 42 American cities. In addition, 181 were open only in the summer months in 85 American cities. During the same year, 37 playgrounds were open for blacks in 28 cities.

The black recreation participation patterns of the 1920s continued through the 1930s. The 1930s saw a steady, yet insufficient increase in the number of outdoor playgrounds in black neighborhoods. In 1938, 34 new year-round playgrounds were constructed, bringing the total number of year-round playgrounds in black neighborhoods to 220. In all, 71 new playgrounds were opened for blacks during that year in 50 cities nationwide.[16] Although this may seem like a lot of new playgrounds, note that this was at the beginning of the playground development movement, so numerous playgrounds were already in use in white communities and more were continually being constructed.

As adolescent and adult blacks were denied access to most public recreation activities, they were forced to provide their own. Many turned to the community pool-room for entertainment. This was alarming because many judges and court workers affirmed that black juvenile delinquency was largely related to lack of appropriate recreation opportunity.[17] Numerous statistics provide solid evidence for these beliefs. In 1937 there were an estimated 21,000,000 youths in the United States. Black youths were estimated to constitute one-twelfth, of the total number or 1,776,666. In the 1930s the benefits and values of recreation for youth were identified, and lack of recreation, or recreation unprofitably used, was thought to have detrimental effects.[18]

The time of year when supervised recreation was offered also had an impact on juvenile problems. More cases of juvenile delinquency were observed when urban playgrounds were not open.[19] This gave rise to recommendations that recreation be available on a year-round basis. If youth were not provided adequate recreation opportunity, they might indulge in activities such as drinking and sexual activity that could have a negative impact on later personality development and social responsibility.

Notes/References

1. Charles S. Johnson. 1930. *The Negro in American Civilization: A Study of Negro Life and Race Relations in the Light of Social Research.* New York: Henry Holt and Company, 304.

2. Benjamin Hunnicutt. 1988. *Work Without End: Abandoning Short Hours for the Right to Work.* Philadelphia: Temple University Press, 114–15.

3. Jessie Carney Smith, ed. 1994. *Black Firsts: 2,000 Years of Extraordinary Achievement.* Detroit, MI: Visible Ink Press, 365.

4. E. B. Henderson. 1940. The participation of Negro youth in community and educational programs. *Journal of Negro Education* 9 (no.3, July): 416–24. Quote is found on 417–18.

5. C. H. Klippel. 1949. Racial integration in the summer camp. *Youth Leaders Digest* (April): 247–49.

6. Henderson.

7. Charles S. Johnson. 1943. *Patterns of Negro Segregation.* New York: Harper and Brothers, 29.

8. Ibid.

9. Johnson, *The Negro,* 330–36; Thomas J. Woofter. 1929. *Negro Problems in Cities.* College Park, MD: McGrath Publishing Company, 228–33.

10. Johnson, *The Negro,* 307.

11. Woofter, 234.

12. Johnson, *The Negro,* 306.

13. Ibid., 299–310.

14. Gunnar Myrdal. 1944. *An American Dilemma: The Negro Problem and Modern Democracy.* New York: Harper and Brothers, 346–47.

15. Johnson, *The Negro,* 299–310.

16. Henderson, 416–24.

17. Woofter, 228.

18. Henderson.

19. Woofter, 228–29.

Chapter Seven

RACE AND PUBLIC RECREATION

Programs of recreation in a community are as broad as the interest of the people and are limited only by the resources of the people, funds, facilities, imagination, and leadership.[1]

E. B. Henderson

Leadership and Professional Supervision of Recreation

There were in general few black children and even fewer black recreation workers on playgrounds in virtually all cities—North or South—in the early part of the twentieth century. In the North and the South black children did not frequent playgrounds. In 1927 Lynchburg, Virginia, had the highest percentage of black children using city playgrounds, an average daily attendance of 508 or 21.6 percent of 3,310 black children. Only Dayton, Ohio, had relatively equal average of its daily participation by black children—500, or 17 percent, of its 2,910 black children. Other cities reported very limited participation by black children on city playgrounds, some as low as 3 percent average daily attendance.[2]

The fact that playgrounds are developed for children's use raises serious questions about the reasons for such low daily participation. One cause might relate to the limited number of blacks employed as playground recreation workers. Considering the general societal attitude at the time, persistent racial discrimination and bias on the part of many whites virtually guaranteed that trained white recreation workers would not provide appropriate recreation services to blacks. Many white recreation workers simply did not want to work with blacks or in black communities. Consequently, municipalities had difficulty getting competent recreation workers who would work with blacks[3] and black adults had difficulty receiving adequate training as professional recreation workers. It was, in fact, not uncommon to find *no* black recreation workers in some major cities. For example, in 1927 Houston, with 3,700 black children, and Atlantic City, with 4,425 black children, employed *no* paid black workers on city playgrounds.[4]

It is likely that those few cities with paid black workers provided little professional training for them. It is also probable that professionally trained leadership was limited even in black communities. The limited number of other early municipal studies of the recreation needs of blacks echoed the broader realities: there was a persistent lack of qualified recreation leadership in black communities. In 1926 the Mayor's Interracial Committee of Detroit, Michigan, reported that the city had increased its provisions from one paid play director in 1915 to five in 1927 and had set aside $268,000 for a recreation center for blacks.

In 1922 T.J. Woofter wrote on race relations in Georgia cities, saying, "In general, Negro playgrounds are less numerous, smaller, poorer in equipment and less adequately supervised than playgrounds for white children in the same cities." This is not difficult to explain. Programs in most instances were not provided because, as Woofter observed, "most of the cities studied have not supplied adequate play space for this group of boys and girls."[5]

Charles Johnson continued his research and wrote the book

The Negro in American Civilization: A Study of Negro Life and Race Relations in Light of Social Research, which provides even more revealing statistics on blacks and public recreation in America. While investigating some of the more heavily populated northern and western cities and states, Johnson's inquiry found, for example:

- that although the census of 1920 indicated that Baltimore, Maryland, had a population of 108,322 blacks and 541,219 whites in the summer of 1926, there were 119 schoolyard leaders for whites and only 17 for blacks.
- that Brooklyn and New York City had no separate playgrounds for blacks.
- that in Harlem, New York, with its high concentration of blacks, there was only one small plot of land used as a playground for African Americans.
- that in Chicago, the most heavily populated city in Illinois, there were four adequately equipped playgrounds, employing 14 recreation leaders, yet none of these playgrounds was located near a black community, so the playgrounds were virtually inaccessible to blacks.

Early in the twentieth century, Detroit was considered one of America's more progressive cities in meeting the recreation needs of all its citizens. More than other cities, Detroit increased its numbers of black recreation directors from one in 1915 to five in 1926. Although at the time Detroit was proud of its seemingly significant accomplishments, considering the percentage of blacks in the city, these increases were very small compared to the increases in the number of white play directors. During the same eleven-year period, Detroit increased its roster of white play directors from 40 in 1915 to 80 in 1926.[6] Much of the lack of adequately trained black recreation workers can be traced to budgets allocated for recreation in black communities and for the hiring and training of black recreation workers. For example, in 1928 Lexington, Kentucky, allocated only $500 of its total $3000 recreation budget for black playgrounds; Charleston, South Carolina, appropriated $360 out of its total recreation budget of $8,975 for playgrounds in black communities. Further, it was common practice for white recreation workers performing similar duties to be paid more than their black counterparts. Interestingly, in 1928 the only southern city with a policy of paying trained black recreation supervisors the same as whites was Winston-Salem, North Carolina.[7]

Libraries

Many personal benefits are gained when individuals read for recreation and/or leisure. Some seek solace, independence, recreation, and leisure in their reading; others read for a sense of accomplishment; still others read for knowledge. For some, a certain element of personal control and competence is gained through recreational reading or reading for pleasure. Reading allows individuals to use their imaginations, which can take them to places they have never been and generate feelings of excitement and contentment.

After slavery, more blacks were "officially" learning to read, but most public libraries did not adequately accommodate them. In 1928 many large cites—including Philadelphia, New York, Chicago, and Indianapolis—had libraries open to all their citizens; however, in line with the southern tradition, blacks were allowed to use only designated parts of these facilities. The most common practice in the South was to have completely separate libraries for blacks and whites.[8] Predictably, blacks were not often afforded the most current reading materials and resources of the library system.

Lacking appropriate access to libraries and to more extensive reading material certainly affected the leisure of African Americans. As new reading material is published, read, and eventually discarded, it becomes outdated, and blacks were not usually privy to published material until it was old and irrelevant. Sometimes they didn't even receive the *outdated* materials. Therefore, blacks could not keep current with new technologies, events, and knowledge.

Reading has been a tool for education, recreation, and leisure since words were first printed. People read books, pamphlets, newspapers, journals, reports, bibles, and so on, but since it was illegal for black slaves to read or write, black Americans fell significantly behind the white majority in reading ability and reading comprehension.

After slavery, blacks were slow to gain access to reading for either education or recreation, since libraries demonstrated significant racial separation and discrimination. Gunnar Myrdal, in his comprehensive broad-based study of blacks in America, found that in 1939 there were 774 public libraries in the southern states. Of that number, only 99 (or fewer than one out of seven) were available to blacks. What is even more interesting is that over half those libraries accessible to blacks were located in only four states: Virginia, Kentucky, Texas, and North Carolina.[9] Only about 21 percent of all blacks had access to a library facility.

Public libraries, especially in the South, were not really *public*. Most made no provisions for black usage, and it was apparent that the educated black person was objectionable to whites, even after emancipation. In most smaller southern cities with one or two libraries, blacks were often prohibited from borrowing books. They were welcome only in the few main branches in selected large cities that were designated as "colored libraries."[10] In the border and northern states the situation was somewhat better: blacks were allowed more freedom in receiving services and were allowed to use more of the public libraries.

This lack of opportunity had lasting effects on blacks. They could not reap the benefits of a medium that communicated thoughts, ideas, philosophy, information, enjoyment, and expression. Without access to libraries, blacks were slow to learn about some recreation and leisure experiences. As America expanded overall access to and engagement in a broader range of recreation and leisure activity, blacks were barred from this process. They had to use the less efficient word-of-mouth method to pass on information to one another. Often, by the time the "word" filtered to the black community, the activity had come and gone, and other popular activities were on the horizon.

Travel literature is one example of this lack of opportunity. As more people began to travel throughout America and the rest of the world, many wrote about their adventures. Blacks were left in the dark about travel possibilities because of their limited access to the written materials on the subject.

Swimming Facilities

As America continued to address its racial problem, social engineers grew concerned with how best to bring the races together.

Initially, they compromised, concluding that blacks and whites surely couldn't eat, sleep, and/or work together in harmony. But could they play together? It seemed a viable option to the PRAA. A committee report at the Third Annual PRAA Congress stated that "the playground is the most democratic influence there is, and race feeling soon fades away in the intimacy of games, unless it is so strong in the beginning as to forbid intercourse, as between white and colored children in the South."[11]

This integration began on a limited basis in parks and in playgrounds with children. In 1940 E.B. Henderson mentioned some of the aims and objectives of private and community recreation programs which included breaking down race, class, and religious prejudices.[12] Early recreation programmers believed that playgrounds and parks could be used to make progress in race relations.

Playing together did not prove too difficult for whites and blacks, and eventually many parks and playgrounds were integrated. However, when blacks were allowed to swim with whites, more serious problems arose. One of the most common points of racial friction in recreation was the utilization of municipal swimming pools and public beaches. Participation in playgrounds and parks allowed blacks and whites flexible involvement, letting the two groups remain physically separate while engaging in the same activities. Psychologically and physically, both could maintain a degree of separateness even at the same facility. Swimming was different. Both races had to use the same water, and that was difficult for some whites to accept because the same water would touch everyone. These feelings rested on white stereotypes about blacks and their cleanliness. Some whites believed that blacks were inherently dirty and might contaminate the swimming water, thereby infecting whites.

A recent television movie dramatically portrays this issue. In *Michael Jordan: An American Hero*, the former basketball star recalls that when he was a young boy, white teammates' parents told them to get out of the swimming pool when Michael and his friends got in.[13] Because he was black, white parents believed their children would "catch something" if they remained in the same pool with Michael. In fact, during Michael's childhood, race relations had actually progressed to a point where whites and blacks felt comfortable competing on some of the same athletic teams. Yet in the swimming pool where there was the perception of closer contact, whites felt threatened. Imagine the impact this had on the development of black youngsters!

It was out of ignorance and racial prejudice that many whites were reluctant to swim, or let their children swim, with blacks. Especially in the South, where prejudice lingered well into the middle part of the twentieth century, many whites defied the law rather than give in to constitutional mandates in this matter. Most municipalities eventually required the desegregation of public recreational facilities, including playgrounds, golf courses, zoos, and parks. However, desegregating public pools was a line in the sand for some whites.

In a Washington, D.C., study published in 1927, Professor William H. Jones of Howard University found that of 25 playgrounds for blacks, only one had a swimming pool.[14] That same year Forrest Washington, director of the Detroit League on Urban Conditions Among Negroes, completed some of the first longitudinal research on the black community. Washington found that in 1927 seventeen southern cities had a *total* of three whites-only (no blacks allowed) bathing beaches and eleven bathing beaches with complete segregation (blacks were restricted to a designated section). Ten public swimming pools were for whites only and six had complete segregation.[15]

There was a similar situation in Chicago. In 1922 Chicago had eight bathing beaches, only three located close to black communities. Nevertheless, whites expected blacks to confine themselves to only *one* beach: Twenty-Sixth Street beach. Twenty-Sixth Street beach did offer access to Lake Michigan, but it was difficult to get to, unattractive in appearance, and lacking the wholesome atmosphere of a recreational beach.[16] By 1940 the swimming pool situation was not much better: there were three inadequate indoor and two outdoor pools for blacks in the nation's capital and some fifty pools for whites.[17]

These statistics offer a context for some of the most famous racial incidents of the early twentieth century. The famous Chicago Riot of 1919 began on July 27, 1919, on the shore of Lake Michigan when a seventeen-year-old black boy drowned at the beach. In the riot 38 persons were killed, 537 injured, and approximately 1,000 rendered homeless.[18] In Chicago blacks and whites had traditionally maintained an imaginary boundary at the public beach. On this particular day, the black youth entered the water in the black section but swam or drifted into the section used by whites. Meanwhile, a disturbance between blacks and whites broke out on the shore. This escalated into stone-throwing, so the youth remained in the water afraid to get out. He was hit by a stone allegedly thrown by a white man, and his death precipitated the deadly riot.

Another of America's most violent race riots occurred in the summer of 1943 on Belle Isle, Detroit's 985-acre playground and beach. That riot claimed the lives of 34 people, and its exact causes were never known. The most common factors leading up to the riot were lack of employment opportunity for blacks; delinquency and crime; racial bigotry and overcrowding in housing, transportation, and recreation.[19] In Detroit that same year, there were a limited number of swimming pools and few playgrounds for blacks. That lack of purposeful recreation opportunity, specifically limited swimming facilities during a hot and humid summer, may also have contributed to the riots.

Pure prejudice and the fear of sexual contact between blacks and whites was a major reason that racial integration at municipal swimming pools and beaches was regarded as abhorrent.[20]

The 1971 case of *Palmer v. Thompson* illustrates the point. In *Palmer*, the court refused by a five-to-four vote to find unconstitutional the decision of Jackson, Mississippi, to close its public swimming pools rather than comply with a court order requiring desegregation of all municipal facilities. In 1962 the city maintained five public swimming pools, four for whites and one for blacks. The Memphis, Tennessee, City Council also decided not to try to operate desegregated public swimming pools, using lack of adequate finances as their primary defense. Subsequently, the council surrendered its lease on one pool and closed the other four. In *Palmer*, white local officials were charged with closing the pool to avoid integration with blacks.[21] Black petitioners brought the action on equal-protection grounds to force the city to reopen and operate desegregated city pools. White officials acknowledged some ideological opposition to pool integration, but their motivation was difficult for a court of law to ascertain. The court indicated that proving discriminatory intent was tough, but it is debatable whether the court felt discriminatory intent was difficult to prove or whether it was reluctant to antagonize the white majority on the issue of racial prejudice, especially when there were more impor-

tant rights—e.g., schooling, jobs, and voting—with a higher prece-
dence in the area of civil rights.

Recreation Facilities, Use, and
Land Allocation in the North:
The Chicago Example

In the early post-slavery years, most of the municipal land provided for recreation for blacks and their communities was inadequate and small in acreage. Data from Chicago, one of America's
largest cities, serves as the basis for much of the following analysis. Chicago has been observed since slavery's end to be one of
the most racially diverse yet segregated cities in America. In 1927
a Chicago Health Survey found that the average ratio of population to each acre of park land was 507:4. However in the second
and third wards of the city, where the population was primarily
black, there was an average population of 8,059 for 9 acres of
park space.[22] This indicates the disparity in park space allocation
between racial communities in the city. Early data is difficult to
locate for most other cities during the same time period, but it is
likely that Chicago was typical of most Northern cities.

During the separate-but-equal period, U.S. cities did not allo-
cate equal recreational acreage for blacks. They were forced to find
their own places for recreation, and they often utilized open spaces
in their neighborhoods. They usually succeeded in adapting local
black churchyards or open fields for their recreation activity.[23] The
problem was more evident in larger cities where the need for facilities was often more pronounced due to the larger black population and the absence of open spaces in black communities.

Again, Chicago may be typical of larger northern cities. In 1922
the city had a total of 127 public places for recreation, including
playgrounds, recreation centers, bathing beaches, and swimming
pools. The municipality had 82 playgrounds, only fourteen of
which were located in black communities, and twenty-nine recreation centers, none of which was located in a black community.[24]
The public facilities most often found in black communities were
playgrounds built for younger children. There was little to attract
and interest older youths except an occasional baseball field.

Only overt and covert racial discrimination can account for the limited facilities and acreage made available to early black communities. Public maintenance of parks and playgrounds was in those days relatively inexpensive, so cost was not the reason for the disparity. There was also relatively little maintenance required for playgrounds: the average maintenance cost in a large metropolitan city like Chicago ranged from about $2,000 to $5,000 annually.

Recreation centers, which were at the time the newest and most notable recreation enterprises, were Chicago's pride and joy. These centers, which allowed participants to play and recreate both inside and outside, represented investments of $300,000 to $800,000 annually in white communities. Citizens could hold meetings or dances, attend concerts, or engage in swimming and numerous other activities at the centers. The basic argument for the development of such centers was that they enhanced wholesome recreation in America. Nevertheless, the argument that wholesome recreation makes for better citizens did not increase the number of recreation centers built in black communities. Consequently, the recreation-center concept was foreign to the black community. Still encumbered by societal conditions of the post-slavery period, blacks did not feel free and were not welcome to attend the centers in white communities.[25]

White officials offered a number of reasons to justify the lack of recreation centers in black communities. For example, they argued that blacks did not want another excuse to be taxed. As one park director stated,

> The law permits acquisition of property for small parks by request of citizens and bond issues for the purchase of the property and its development. When it comes to maintenance the question of taxes comes in, and unless people are willing to be taxed in excess of what they are taxed now, there won't be any possibility of maintaining more parks.[26]

Obviously, there was a lack of understanding on the part of white municipal officials about what blacks needed, wanted, and were willing to pay for.

Southern Recreation Opportunity for Blacks

If the opportunity in the North was substandard, in the South the disparity was even more pronounced. In many southern cities, the park space provided for black recreation was minuscule. In 1927 Nashville, Tennessee, had a population that was 28 percent black, but the city allocated only about 1 percent of its total park space to its black citizens.[27] The pattern of limited municipal park space allocation continued into the following decades. As late as 1940 Raleigh, North Carolina, had a population of 31,061 whites and 15,818 blacks, but had only three playgrounds, one park with a swimming pool, and one community center for all its black citizens. In the same year Greensboro, North Carolina, had a population of 42,968 whites and 16,343 blacks, but had only one park with a swimming pool, a golf course, and one playground for its black citizens. Imagine having more than 16,000 people using one playground and swimming pool in the hot and humid North Carolina summer! Winston-Salem had the largest black population in North Carolina (36,000 in 1940) and had *no* special recreational facilities for blacks except a single swimming pool. Knoxville, Tennessee, had a population of 98,657 whites and 13,310 blacks, but blacks had access to only 2 of the city's 14 playgrounds and were not allowed to use any of its parks. In Waco, Texas, the situation was no better. Waco, Texas, had a population of 7,726 blacks and 28,995 whites, but only two playgrounds and none of the parks could be used by blacks.[28] These findings illustrate serious deficiencies in public recreation facilities for black communities in the days of separate-but-equal in the South.

Notes/References

1. E.B. Henderson. 1940. The participation of Negro youth in community and educational programs. *Journal of Negro Education* 9 (no. 3, July): 416–24.

2. Charles S. Johnson. 1930. *The Negro in American Civilization: A Study of Life and Race Relations in the Light of Social Research.* New York: Henry Holt and Company, 301.

3. Thomas J. Woofter. 1929. *Negro Problems in Cities.* College Park, MD: McGrath Publishing Company, 236.

4. Johnson, 301.

5. Cited in Johnson (1930), 307.

6. Johnson, 305.

7. Woofter, 237.

8. Ibid.

9. Gunnar Myrdal. 1944. *An American Dilemma: The Negro Problem and Modern Democracy*. New York: Harper and Brothers Publishers, 344.

10. Charles S. Johnson. 1943. *Patterns of Negro Segregation*. New York: Harper and Brothers, 26.

11. Proceedings of the Third Annual Congress of the PRAA. 1909. Pittsburgh, PA, May 10–14. From the Report of the Committee on a Normal Course of Play, p. 139. National Recreation Association (NRA) Collection, Social Welfare History Archives, University of Minnesota, Minneapolis.

12. Henderson., 417–24.

13. *Michael Jordan: An America Hero*. 1999. Produced by Michael J. Murray, based on the book by Jim Naughton. Avalanche Home Entertainment, VHS and DVD.

14. Johnson (1930), 306.

15. Ibid., 303.

16. William M. Tuttle Jr. 1970. *Race Riot: Chicago in the Red Summer of 1919*. New York: Atheneum, 3.

17. Henderson, 418.

18. Chicago Commission on Race Relations. 1922. *The Negro in Chicago: A Study of Race Relations and a Race Riot in 1919*. Chicago: University of Chicago Press, 1.

19. Alfred M. Lee. 1943. *Race Riot, Detroit 1943*. New York: Dryden Press, 88–97.

20. Stephan Thernstrom and Abigail Thernstrom. 1997. *America in Black and White*. New York: Simon & Schuster, 42.

21. *Palmer v. Thompson*. 1971. 403 U.S. 217, 224. Cited in Derrick Bell. 1987. *And We Are Not Saved: The Elusive Quest for Racial Justice*. New York: Basic Books, 172.

22. Johnson (1930), 306.

23. Johnson (1943), 29.

24. Chicago Commission on Race Relations, 272.

25. Ibid., 273.

26. Chicago Commission on Race Relations, 273–74.

27. Johnson (1943), 29.

28. Johnson 299–310.

Chapter 8

BLACKS AND
COMMERCIAL RECREATION

After the war many of the prejudices and traditions of slavery lingered on in both the North and the South. Richard Kraus, one of the best known writers on the history of recreation and leisure, wrote of the period, ". . . citizens of color [blacks] were extremely limited in their use of organized recreation and park facilities."[1] Primarily in the South, but also in the North, there was racial discrimination and segregation in private, commercial, and public recreation facilities. Everywhere in the South strict segregation and discrimination prohibited blacks from using public recreational facilities like libraries, public parks and playgrounds, and even many commercial recreational establishments such as hotels and restaurants.[2] When public recreation was not available to them even in the larger southern and some northern cities, blacks were forced to turn to private commercial recreation. However, private enterprise was left free to exploit the recreation market, leaving often debasing, usually more expensive and less desirable alternatives open to black citizens.[3] The size and/or location of the city made very little difference. In large and small cities and rural areas, recreational activities, facilities, and support for blacks were universally inadequate. These inequalities were initially identified in commercial recreation.

Eating and Traveling

Even in areas where consumers pay for services rendered, racial discrimination prevailed. This had a definitive impact on the recreation and leisure activities of blacks. Most blacks were poor, and even those who could afford to travel for recreation often found themselves significantly hampered. Imagine being able to pay for a service and then not being allowed to obtain the service due to racial segregation and prejudice. Discrimination was endemic in most commercial recreation establishments like hotels and restaurants. The lack of black opportunity was most often attributed to lack of access to transportation and the inaccessibility of housing (hotels and motels) and dining facilities.

Most blacks who dared travel outside their immediate communities, especially in the South, had to make arrangements to stay in private homes or black schools because white hotels would not accommodate them. There were few if any black-owned and operated hotels in the South, and many blacks did not feel comfortable outside the familiar surrounding communities. Especially in the rural South, many churches would provide lodging for black travelers.[4]

In the northern and border states, the temporary boarding situation was somewhat better because there were a few more black-owned or -operated hotels. However, the number of black-owned hotels and motels was very limited everywhere in America. A few blacks of "national reputation" might be allowed to stay at white-owned and -operated hotels in the North, provided agreements and arrangements were made in advance. Such arrangements might require black guests to enter and exit the hotel as inconspicuously as possible so that the local white citizens would not know they were staying at the establishment.[5]

Commercial eating establishments also practiced tremendous segregation and discrimination.[6] This was particularly important because it was difficult for blacks to travel any extended distance or length of time without access to food. In the South, some white-owned restaurants whose clientele was white might allow blacks to enter through a side or back door and be served in the kitchen, yet even this was an exception to the rule. Sometimes if blacks were served in white establishments, they had to take their food elsewhere to eat.

Even in the North where more equal opportunity was thought to exist, blacks had to be selective in choosing places to eat outside the black community. Many northern white-operated eating establishments discouraged black patronage. This was a matter of the managerial preference of the individual establishment and of the particular circumstances under which service was being sought. That made it difficult to predict what would happen to blacks seeking meal service outside their home communities[7] anywhere in America.

This discrimination in lodging and eating would have lasting effects on blacks and their recreation and leisure. Most blacks were more or less forced to find social and recreation activity close to their homes. Since travel itself is often viewed as a form of recreation and as a means of access to other leisure pursuits, black opportunity was very much affected by segregation.

Not only did blacks fear what they would find regarding lodging and meals when they reached their travel destinations, they also met with inequality and discrimination in the separate-but-equal transportation system itself. As with lodging and eating, blacks feared travel because of potential encounters with racism and prejudice.

During the Jim Crow years, there was a definite caste system under which blacks were expected to conduct themselves as the lowest caste. One problem was that behavior perfectly acceptable in one state or town could be a violation of accepted behavior in others. So blacks had to be careful when venturing into unfamiliar territory,[8] especially if they had to rely on public transportation.

All southern states had laws separating whites and blacks in transportation—on trains, on buses, and in taxicabs. Although the law of the land was separate-but-equal, there was little or no equality. Railroad companies were supposed to provide equal, separate sleeping and dining cars for whites and blacks. This seldom if ever happened. Blacks were usually confined to the oldest, worst-equipped, and filthiest train cars.

Probably the best documented cases of inequality for blacks in transportation involved city buses. City buses were used for transportation to work, shopping, visiting, and other appointments, and for travel to recreation and leisure destinations. When city buses were first introduced in the South, bus companies had no apparent plans to provide equal space for blacks, so buses in many cities initially accepted only white passengers. Individual states and cities took action to allow greater access for blacks. For example, legal action was undertaken in North Carolina to allow blacks to ride public buses.

When blacks were eventually allowed to ride the buses, they were to fill the bus from the rear while whites filled it from the front. Generally, there was no legal dividing line between the front and the back of a bus. Some cities, like Houston, Texas, used movable signs to designate racial sections. In these instances bus drivers could alter seating arrangements depending on the number of white passengers. In other cases, seating boundaries were determined by the route a bus traveled. For example, if the bus made its rounds in a black neighborhood, blacks were allowed seating throughout the bus. They might also sit wherever they wanted on the bus as long as they left the first two seats open for whites. It was the famous 1955 incident involving Rosa Parks that put an end to such discriminatory practices.

Other Commercial and Private Recreation

In other commercial recreation activities, segregation and discrimination were also present. Some of the more prominent commercial entertainments of the day were offered in motion picture theaters, vaudeville houses, amusement parks, and theaters. Southern cities were characterized by significantly more whites-only (completely segregated) facilities than those in the North. For whites, the most popular commercial amusements in the early part of the twentieth century included movie theaters, swimming pools, skating rinks, bowling alleys, dance halls, and baseball parks. Blacks were virtually excluded from all these facilities except theaters, baseball parks, and vaudeville houses.[9] In most cities where blacks were allowed in baseball parks and vaudeville establishments, separate seating for blacks and whites was the rule.

Even cities with large numbers of blacks offered them very limited commercial recreation opportunities, and most of these were indoor amusements. Since there was no public recreation offered to black communities, blacks had to rely more on commercial amusements. Detroit, with a black population of approximately 35,000 in 1915, had only one motion-picture theatre located near the largest black neighborhood.

In many cities the principal amusement places for black men were pool-rooms, often termed pool parlors.[10] There was little recreation for black females. Black males felt comfortable in pool-rooms. Since these establishments required relatively little capital investment, some entrepreneurial blacks bought and/or managed local community pool parlors. These were popular for a number of reasons. In the early part of the century, they provided a social environment where blacks could come together with others outside their immediate families. At billiards blacks could show their talents and compete against others with similar interests. Unfortunately, other sometimes illegitimate, activities such as gambling and prostitution were also available. These pursuits could hardly be considered wholesome recreation. They were illegal and they helped erode the urban black community's quality of life. In 1940 E.B. Henderson commented on the negative effects of the community pool-room by stating that these establishments attracted a large measure of the lawless as well as innocent seekers of harmless recreation. In effect, pool-rooms became socially dangerous[11] in many black communities.

Especially in rural black communities in the 1930s and 1940s, it was easier to find places to drink alcohol than to find places for supervised recreation. In cities like Detroit, black community organizations were largely responsible for providing commercial social recreation. The Detroit Urban League sponsored many activities including dances, since dancing continued to be a favorite pastime for blacks. Charging minimal admission, these events were largely successful. Any surplus revenue was used to promote other community activities such as baseball, basketball, and the Boy and Girl Scouts.[12]

Even though white commercial recreation facilities stood to profit by accepting blacks, most were reluctant to integrate. Racial bigotry definitely outweighed the desire for financial profits. Some more entrepreneurial whites sometimes opened establishments in black communities which were run by blacks while the white owners reaped their profits.

Improving Black Recreation Opportunity

African Americans, like all human beings, need to remain actively engaged in life. Recreation and leisure are deeply ingrained in the black psyche. African Americans have always recognized the benefits of healthy and wholesome recreation, even prior to their arrival in America. The fact that the country did not adequately provide what was needed did not deter blacks from seeking their own recreation and leisure satisfaction.

At a time of legal segregation and unequal recreation facility availability, how did blacks begin to acquire some shares of the pie? The most consistent method of securing recreation services was through private financing. In short, blacks were forced to purchase selected recreation services with their own monies. However, in a separatist society blacks had a strong claim on municipal services supported by federal and local funds. In most cases, legal action and formal protest secured improvements in segregated services.[13] The most disturbing aspect of this situation is that blacks had to turn to the courts simply to secure their basic American rights.

For example, golf was closed to most blacks. Charles Johnson investigated this fact and wrote that in Chicago, "A few Negroes play golf at the Lincoln Park public golf course." Individuals in Washington, D.C., Philadelphia, Minneapolis, Detroit, and New York also registered specific objections against blacks playing golf on their public courses.[14] In the early 1950s Houston, Portsmouth, and Louisville were ordered by the courts to provide "equal facilities" for black golfers.[15] In an effort to comply with the law, some cities offered piecemeal solutions such as allowing blacks to play on a few specific days of the week. Obviously, golf was not the recreation service most needed by blacks, but it provided a clear case of discrimination in public facilities. Nonetheless, these provisional golf privileges extended to restrictions on recreational activities such as baseball, tennis, and fishing.

Protest carried its own problems for blacks. They had to carefully weigh the potential benefits and losses which could result from a protest. Individual bigotry might distort judicial decision making and hamper the cause of humanitarian righteousness. In some cases, therefore, blacks, were reluctant to risk the incremental gains they'd made—particularly those related to segregated facility usage—and had to think twice before protesting segregation in public facilities. Too strong a protest in one area could mean losses in other important areas.[16] Blacks had to decide if a protest was worth the risk of losing a facility altogether and at the same time (considering the racial climate of the period) engendering further animosity from any whites who would lose their public facilities because of black protests.

Through pressure from the courts, petitions, protest, and public hearings, a gradual increase began in opening public city parks and swimming facilities to black citizens. For example, in Birmingham, Alabama, between 1943 and 1948, blacks gained seven city parks.[17] After legal action was taken in the middle of the century with separate-but-equal in place, *some* improvements were made in *some* segregated facilities. In Virginia, after two years of court battles, the first state park for blacks was completed in 1950, though the state simultaneously operated eight other state parks for white citizens. In the same year South Carolina voted for funds for a new state park for blacks and for improvements in the black section of an existing park. Other court decisions eventually gave blacks access to public beaches and bath houses, golf courses, and other facilities.

Similar tactics were used to address the discrimination posed in municipalities and libraries. However, inequities remained. America needed to guarantee equitable rights for all its citizens. The public recreation profession, attempting to be more assertive in this period of enlightenment, sought out competent individuals to assist in this effort.

Notes/References

1. Richard Kraus. 1997. *Recreation and Leisure in Modern Society*, 5th ed. Menlo Park, CA: Addison Wesley Longman, 199.

2. Charles S. Johnson. 1943. *Patterns of Negro Segregation*. New York: Harper and Brothers, 56.

3. George S. Schuyler. 1929. Keeping the Negro in his place. *American Mercury* 17, no. 68 (August): 469–76.

4. Arthur Raper. 1936. *Preface to Peasantry: A Tale of Two Black Belt Counties*. Chapel Hill, NC: University of North Carolina Press, 373.

5. Johnson, 58.

6. Raper, 384–85.

7. Johnson, 57–63

8. Stephan Thernstrom and Abigail Thernstrom. 1997. *America in Black and White*. New York: Simon & Schuster, 44.

9. Johnson, 72.

10. G. E. Haynes. 1918. *Negro New-Comers in Detroit, Michigan: A Challenge to Christian Statesmanship—A Preliminary Survey*. New York: Home Missions Council, 25.

11. E. B. Henderson. 1940. The participation of Negro youth in community and educational programs. *Journal of Negro Education* 9, no.3 (July): p. 423.

12. Haynes, 25.

13. Jessie P. Guzman, ed. 1952. *1952 Negro Yearbook*. New York: Wm. H. Wise & Co., 316.

14. Charles J. Johnson. 1930. *The Negro in American Civilization: A Study of Negro Life and Race Relations in the Light of Social Research*. New York: Henry Holt and Company, 303.

15. Guzman, 316.

16. *Palmer v. Thompson*, 403 U.S. 217 (1971). Cited in Derrick A. Bell. 1987. *And We Are Not Saved: The Elusive Quest for Racial Justice*. New York: Basic Books, 172.

17. Guzman, 316.

Chapter 9

BLACK RECREATION IN FOCUS

Funding for Black Recreation:
Obtaining Financial Support

Gaining adequate funding for play, recreation, and leisure has always been an issue for citizens and for the recreation profession itself. This was especially true for blacks. Obtaining funding for recreation in black communities proved particularly difficult. Traditionally, financial support for public recreation was derived primarily from municipal funds. In the 1920s, however, some cities received funding from other sources: in Denver and Philadelphia, from boards of education; in Baltimore, half from a community fund; in Houston, from both the city council and a community fund.[1] Still, the recreation profession relied heavily on municipal financing. Within this funding structure, the basic philosophy was that all citizens of a community are taxed to pay for services rendered to the entire city, not just to the section of the city where a given citizen lives. The system's basic tenet is that everyone shares in equal services available to all citizens of the community.

This did not work for black communities. Most public funding for public recreation went to whites-only facilities, leaving blacks with little or no financial resources to procure and enhance facilities. Seldom were black neighborhoods allocated anything close to their equal and adequate proportion of the funds.

Realizing the value of play and recreation for the community, members of the black community clung to the dream of more recreation opportunities in their neighborhoods, but they had to resort to other means to fund that recreation. For example, they sought "community chest" support meaning that community members made voluntary contributions. Although some funds were collected, this method proved largely ineffective. The majority of blacks were poor, so their collective effort did not produce significant revenue.

Still convinced of the value of recreation, many blacks turned entrepreneurs. Some opened pool-rooms,[2] others organized plays, musical programs, and social gatherings, drawing on local black talent. The money raised proved to be a major source of revenue for their recreation.

Nevertheless, these efforts did not always result in substantial improvements because black community resources were extremely limited. Many citizens would not contribute until time or tradition demonstrated the benefits of a program or facility for the community. Nevertheless, there were other beneficial by-products. These fundraising efforts sometimes brought together important black and white leaders, fostering better race relations.

Much of the recreational funding, particularly for activities for children and youth, was provided by churches or by voluntary agencies affiliated with local community clubs such as the Young Men's Christian Association (YMCA) and the Young Women's Christian Association (YWCA). Many such clubs operated on voluntary financing and volunteer workers.[3]

The YMCAs, or Ys, offered special opportunity for recreation in black communities. Since blacks were not welcome in most white recreation facilities, they flocked to their community YMCAs.[4] The Y was often the place where blacks learned such skills as swimming.

Indeed, had it not been for the Y, many blacks would never have learned to swim. Like the Y, the black churches also took the lead in providing recreation for the black community.

The Black Church and Recreation

> Among most people the primitive sociological group was the family or at least the clan . . . Not so among American Negroes; such vestiges of primitive organization were destroyed by the slaveship. In this country the first distinct voluntary organization of Negroes was the Negro Church. The Negro church came before the Negro home; it ante-dates their social life, and in every respect it stands to-day as the fullest, broadest expression of organized Negro life . . . The Negro church is not simply an organism for the propagation of religion; it is the center of social, intellectual and religious life of individuals. It provides social intercourse, it provides amusements of various kinds, it serves as a newspaper and intelligence bureau, it supplants the theatre, it directs the picnic and excursion, it furnishes the music, it introduces the stranger to the community; it serves as lyceum, library, and lecture bureau; it is, in fine, the central organ of the organized life of the American Negro for amusement, relaxation, instruction and religion."(Dubois, 1899)[5]

Dubois' comments point to the importance of the black church after the slavery period. To be sure, the black community was comfortable. It protected blacks, and blacks *needed* protection in an otherwise hostile society. When they left their communities, they proceeded cautiously, often eating or using the bathroom before they left home so they would not have to use restaurants or bathroom facilities in white areas. Many blacks did all their shopping in their home neighborhoods because they did not have the transportation to go to major shopping areas or because they feared negative contact with whites.[6] Community groups were influential in providing recreation in urban areas, but the churches were most effective. A number of church groups and organizations, including the Methodist Church's Bureau of Town and Country Work, the Congregational-Christian Churches American Missionary Association, the Catholic Church, the Church of the

Brethren, the Quakers, the Town and Country Church of the Evangelical and Reformed Church, and the National Town-Country Episcopal Church[7] offered social welfare services to some black communities.

After slavery many blacks had moved into urban areas where they continued to face prejudice. Such treatment resulted in limited occupational opportunity, so that—especially in larger urban areas—blacks were forced into a limited number of occupations, many of them manual-labor-factory positions or service jobs. Service positions included waiters, train porters, bus-boys, and housekeepers. Housekeeping was often dreaded. It was a low-paying job and most blacks needed more money. Housekeeping also meant cleaning the homes of whites, an occupation with a social stigma based on memories of slavery. Many blacks wanted to be far removed from any form of servitude. Furthermore, the work of housekeeping typically entailed a certain monotony, dullness, and repetition, and was not as reliable as some forms of manual labor—yet it often demanded more of the worker's overall time.[8] Finally, there was little if any room for career advancement in housekeeping.

The church played an important part in relieving the monotony of life for black domestic employees after slavery. With a limited amount of leisure time and little to do when they were not working, many blacks turned to the church for recreation. This role of the church was reaffirmed by W. E. B. Dubois in the results of his classic study *The Philadelphia Negro: A Social Study*. In a survey of more than 10,000 Philadelphia residents in 1897 three-quarters of respondents indicated they got their amusements and recreation from their churches.[9] Yet the quality of the services provided by black churches suffered from the same limitations as volunteer agencies in American urban areas: limited budgets, inadequate facilities, and limited numbers of persons who could be adequately served.

Since its inception in Philadelphia in 1816 when free blacks established Bethel Church of the African Methodist Episcopal (AME) denomination, the black church was central in the lives of black citizens. The church became the center of black community life and provided a certain autonomy for its members. Churches offered many of the services which public enterprises neglected. It was a sanctuary of freedom for blacks in an otherwise hostile world. The white man's respect for religion freed the black church from the imposition of limitations and restrictions otherwise routinely imposed on its people.

The location of the church also made it an attractive community center. Most black churches were located at the center of black communities, readily accessible to the many blacks who lacked transportation for long-distance travel. The church was accommodating to its members and a number of black groups used churches as meeting places. Many black community fraternal organizations, including clubs and lodges, met in the local black church. In addition, the church was used as a place for civic meetings and discussion of community issues.

As most public social centers were closed to blacks, the black church was often the only place where business and socialization could be conducted. As Carter G. Woodson stated:

> Negroes regularly attend church whether Christians or sinners. They have not yet accumulated wealth adequate to the construction of clubhouses, amusement parks, and theaters, although dance halls have attracted many. Whether they derive any particular joy therefrom or not, the Negroes must go to church, to see their friends, as they are barred from social centers open to whites. They must attend church moreover, to find out what is going on; for the race has not sufficient interests to maintain in every locality a newspaper of its own, and the whites generally mention Negroes only when they happen to commit crimes against white persons. The young Negro must go to the church to meet his sweetheart, to impress her with his worth and woo her into marriage, the Negro farmer to find developments in the business world, the Negro mechanic to learn the needs of his community and how he may supply them.[10]

While municipal funding for black recreation was generally limited, the black church became the leader in providing this outlet. Especially in the rural South where there were few public buildings for black recreation, the church was the community centerpiece. Only in some of the larger southern cities could one find a publicly funded recreation center for blacks. When these were found, they were generally provided by private enterprise.[11]

In the larger black urban churches, the social and recreation opportunities provided were quite broad. The black community needed the church's perspective, and many black churches—especially those that could afford to be accommodating—met the black communities' recreation needs. In 1933 Benjamin Mays and Joseph Nicholson, in their book *The Negro Church*, surveyed 609 black churches and found the following resources and activities offered:

- Clubs (Social, Educational, Financial)
- Poor relief
- Recreational work
- Gymnasium classes
- Motion pictures
- Cooperative YW and YMCAs, Girl Scouts, and Boy Scouts
- Music classes[12]

Clearly, these activities expanded the boundaries of the churches' mission.

W. E B. DuBois also observed that the church routinely provided entertainment and amusements including concerts, suppers, socials, fairs, literary exercises and debates, cantatas, plays, trips and excursions, picnics, surprise parties, and numerous celebrations.[13] In practically every black church there was some activity offered throughout the week. The church was meeting needs of its members that were not met by public or other private entities. Nevertheless, since the church was owned and operated by its black members, the programs offered were generally confined to activities approved and regulated by the church.

The church was governed by a moral code that called for a certain level of control over the character of recreation in the church. The Methodist and Baptist churches, to which most blacks belonged, imposed stringent rules of moral conduct. For example, certain activities were generally not allowed in churches: card-playing, dancing, gambling, some sporting activities, and some picnics.[14] As such, individual recreational and leisure preferences might be missing from the church's agenda.

The church as a community recreation facility made an important contribution to the activity options of blacks by providing recreational opportunities for different age and gender groups. These activities included social service recreational endeavors that may have reduced adult and juvenile delinquency in the black community and elsewhere. In this light, the church was instrumental in developing and maintaining a unified sense of community. There were few public places where blacks could feel truly at ease. Among the most common of these were the church, the barbershop, and the pool parlor.

The place where people got their hair cut and styled was unique in the black community. Its importance can be traced back to slavery. In these places, there was frequent conversation that stimulated the mind, local events were discussed and promoted, and friendships were begun and renewed.

Clearly the church, like the barbershop and pool parlor, was a place to go for socialization and recreation in the black community. But the church was more than the pool parlor or the barbershop: the church was the hallmark of the black community. With effective leadership, the church was the pride and joy of the community, and most blacks were guided by its principles.

The Harlem Renaissance

In March 1924 Charles S. Johnson, a respected black sociologist was in New York City completing longitudinal research on blacks in urban America. He organized a dinner with some local dignitaries, an event unofficially recognized as the beginning of the Harlem Renaissance.[15] Johnson and his constituents saw that there were fewer prejudicial obstacles for blacks in selected areas of American life, including publishing and entertainment.[16] In these areas, therefore, they orchestrated a concentrated focus for the African-American community. The Harlem Renaissance generated an incredible aura of confidence and creativity for African Americans in the 1920s. The word *renaissance* encompasses the broadness and complexity of the cultural and creative genius of African Americans. African Americans have produced substantial numbers of artists, writers, musicians, orators, dramatists, and entertainers—e.g., Langston Hughes, Zora Neal Hurston, Sterling Brown, Paul Lawrence Dunbar, Maya Angelou, and Gwendolyn Brooks.[17] Many blacks involved in these vocations became influential in the recreation and leisure of all Americans. Until this point whites had succeeded in limiting the progress of talented African Americans in most areas of life.

Bridging the Gap:
Ernest Attwell and the NRA

The previous section explains some of the specific issues regarding blacks and their opportunity and involvement in the early recreation movement. It was increasingly apparent that more effective leadership was needed at the national level in order to bridge the gap of recreation opportunity in America. How was this to occur in a period of such obvious discrimination? The National Recreation Association (which later became the National Recreation and Park Association) was the organization that met this challenge.

The unofficial national recreation movement began in 1898 when twenty-six city park superintendents met in Boston to discuss professional issues. Some eight years later, in 1906, the Playground and Recreation Association of America (PRAA) was established. The PRAA began working with white communities in 1906. Because public supervised recreation was a new concept for Americans, the PRAA's initial efforts tested the social climate for acceptance of this new recreation initiative. In Memphis, Tennessee, plans for playgrounds and social centers were delayed until the effects of these facilities on whites could be determined.[18] As a result, the association provided organized and supervised play areas and social centers for whites, especially working class whites, well before black interest and needs were addressed.

Prior to 1906 the PRAA had been conforming to the controversial request of many of its founders for reform and control. The PRAA was funded in its formative years primarily through gifts from industrial philanthropists. The primary reason for this support was to foster citizenship, democracy, and control.[19] This control was rationalized as necessary in light of the increase in projected American leisure time as a result of corporate industrialism and urban expansion. In a rapidly changing America, reformers sought to alleviate the potential negative consequences of society with time on its hands. Consequently, recreation and recreational facilities were created to provide organized, safe, and properly supervised leisure activities for as many citizens as possible.

Not until 1926, some sixty-one years after slavery and five years after hiring its first black field director, did the PRAA begin actively promoting recreation programs for African Americans.[20]

Thomas Parker, a white millionaire from Greenville, South Carolina, confirmed in 1924 at the Eleventh PRAA Congress,

> We got in touch with the PRAA, and . . . mapped out a plan, secured money form the City Council, raised some more privately, built four of five playgrounds, and employed a very capable worker . . . Of course, we hadn't thought of the colored people of the city. The playgrounds were for whites.

Parker went on to admit,

> In Greenville, business men took no active interest (in the black citizenry) until they commenced to feel the pinch of migration. The Chamber of Commerce formed an inter-racial committee of its prominent citizens. Those citizens very quickly realized that . . . we knew very little about the negroes, except that we employed them.[21]

The PRAA's involvement in the interests and needs of blacks and their recreation was not voluntary. Only after the pressures of war, migration, Jim Crow laws, and urban violence attracted national attention did the PRAA seek to intervene.[22]

In the early part of the century, a wide variety of organizations had been formed by citizen groups and nonprofessional organizations to meet society's recreation needs. These organizations included

- the National Recreation Association,
- the American Institute of Park Executives,
- the Association of Zoological Parks and Aquariums,
- the American Recreation Society,
- the National Conference on State Parks,
- the National Association of Recreation Therapists,
- the Armed Forces Section of the American Recreation Society.

In 1965 these groups consolidated to form the National Recreation and Park Association .[23]

The National Recreation and Park Association actually traces its beginnings to the late 1800s.[24] Earlier, the National Recreation Association had been the leader in addressing society's broad recreation needs. Some of the organization's early leaders were responsible for the imagination, vision, and action that caused recreation to be recognized as an important basic human need. Some of the most influential individuals in the profession's early years included Joseph Lee, Luther Gulick, Dorothy Enderis, Beatrice Hill, Josephine Randall, and Henry Curtis,[25] among others. Each of these professionals excelled in his or her accomplishments and in the desire to lead the profession through the early stages of organizational development, yet none was capable of successfully addressing the race issue: the issue of how to accommodate black interests, involvement, access, and participation in recreation in a white majority society. To solve this dilemma, the Association sought the expertise of Ernest Teneyck Attwell.

In 1923, Ernest Attwell wrote:

> We should not overlook the handicap of not having play-space or playgrounds where colored people live. The need almost overshadowing the other activities is a recreational program that can be both educational and cultural, such as the inclusion of and participation in community service, dramatic and literary activities that for the large mass of adults will be the only attractive phase of the recreation field.
>
> These latter activities are phases of social life which colored people are greatly in need of. Except for a limited and favored group, social recreation is largely of the commercial and unwholesome type, or to say the least conducted in an atmosphere of moral haze.[26]

Ernest T. Attwell was one of the most influential black professionals involved in the early recreation movement. He was without question largely responsible for securing additional and better recreation opportunities for blacks and their communities in the early part of the century. Indeed, the PRAA did not seriously address the recreation needs of blacks and their communities until 1919 when Attwell joined its staff. In March of that year, Attwell was invited to join the staff of the association with the primary objective of heading its newly formed Bureau of Colored Work. Under mounting pressure based on democratic principles, the primary purpose of this bureau was to expand the association's supervised recreation opportunities, facilities, and leadership available to blacks, and to encourage more black participation in the association's public recreation programs. Through the leadership of Attwell, significant numbers of community centers and playgrounds were built in black communities and more African-American recreation leaders were given professional training.

Why did the association choose Attwell? He was appointed to head the bureau because of his previous involvement and success in a number of high-ranking professional and academic positions, including serving as Assistant to the Food Administrator in Alabama (a position in the U.S. Food Administration Department) and teaching and coaching at Tuskeegee Institute. As will be discussed later, it was at Tuskeegee under the close guidance of its founder Booker T. Washington that Attwell developed much of the personal and professional philosophy which enhanced his ability to act as a successful liaison between the white and black races. Attwell accepted the reality of segregation, a philosophy which was in harmony with the dominant political orientation of the time. In 1921 he wrote that Macon, Georgia, "aims to provide equal recreation facilities for white and colored, three being for white playgrounds and one colored. Reports show that the recent establishment of the latter is appreciated."[27] Using Attwell's philosophy the association ensured a sense of cooperation between black and white community leaders.

Attwell was proficient and professional, and his sphere of influence was broad. He was especially effective at assisting local finance campaigns for the funding of recreation facilities for blacks, such as playgrounds, recreation buildings, swimming pools, and golf courses.[28] He knew the importance of building social relationships and advocated for more than simply constructing parks and playgrounds. As a result, he was instrumental in the development of community centers where blacks could make more substantial social contacts. These centers not only provided recreation activities but also commonly included libraries, nurseries, health-care centers, and other services aimed at helping black neighborhoods. Attwell fought for additional recreational programs for blacks after observing that of the nearly 4,000 play centers reported in 1927, a mere 147 were being used exclusively by black children.

Much of Attwell's success was in providing urban recreation opportunity. He was one of the first to advance the notion that adequate recreation opportunities may be a deterrent to delinquency in the inner cities. The recruitment, training, and placement of black recreation leaders ranked high among Mr. Attwell's objectives and achievements. Attwell spent a considerable portion of his time trying to improve the quality and number of black recreation leaders. On an annual basis he conducted extended workshops in cities around the country, teaching the recreation philosophy for blacks for a minimum fee.[29] This method was very useful because most colleges were not offering recreation courses, and the few that did were not accepting black students.

Attwell was also an effective teacher of whites in the recreation profession. His advice and counsel "were eagerly sought by municipal officials and lay civic leaders, both white and colored, struggling with . . . the complex problem of recreation for the colored citizens."[30] He served on the faculty of the National Recreation School (of the PRAA) throughout its existence, when practically all of its students were white. Many white graduates of the school gained much from his lectures, especially later in their professional careers when they had to deal with blacks and the problems of race in recreation. One of Attwell's early responsibilities was reporting on the status of black recreation opportunity to the PRAA. It should be noted that prior to Attwell, there were *no* publicly organized programs for blacks. Thus, one of Attwell's first reports to the PRAA indicated that only about 3 percent of all the playgrounds then operated in America beckoned black inhabitants to participate in public recreation activities.[31]

While Attwell directed the Playground Association of America in 1927, he developed a policy for how a city program should be organized. He believed that plans should include opportunities for all groups of citizens.[32] Yet while making advances for urban blacks, he also encouraged recreational opportunities for rural towns, implying that they too were in dire need of recreation programming. He was a strong proponent of interracial interest in recreation procurement. In addition, he advocated training of more black leaders for the recreation profession.

The Hampton-Tuskegee Model

Attwell's work with the bureau went on during the separate-but-equal period. E. T. Attwell accepted the separation of the races as a given in his struggle to provide recreational facilities and leadership to blacks.[33] He believed that blacks, in terms of recreation activities, represented a community within a community. Perhaps the greatest insight into understanding Attwell relates to his college education under the Hampton-Tuskegee educational model. Booker T. Washington founded Tuskegee Normal and Industrial Institute, a black higher education institution, in 1881, about fifteen years after the official end of slavery. Washington was a devoted follower of Samuel Chapman Armstrong who founded Hampton Institute in 1868 and who was primarily responsible for the initiation of the Hampton-Tuskegee model.

The Hampton-Tuskeegee model is a conceptual idea, a theory of how blacks should be educated after slavery. This model was not centered on trade or agricultural training; rather, the model centered on the training of teachers. Black teachers would provide leadership for the next generation of blacks in America. The model prescribed a rigorous routine of manual labor designed to teach students steady work habits, practical knowledge, and Christian morals. More importantly, this model viewed industrial education primarily as an ideological force that could help blacks adjust to a subordinate role in the emergent New South. In his book *The Education of Blacks in the South, 1860–1935*, James Anderson, a professor of education at the University of Illinois, stated, "Hampton developed an extensive manual labor routine because the school's faculty believed that a particular combination of hard work, political socialization, and social discipline would mold appropriately conservative black teachers."[34]

Armstrong and to a lesser extent Washington felt that the removal of black people from any effective role in southern politics was the first step toward proper reconstruction. In particular, Armstrong wrote almost exclusively of the immorality and irresponsibility of black voters and even went so far as to publicly say that black leaders should stay out of politics because they were not capable of self-government. Armstrong's political campaign was based on the notion that whites were mentally and morally strong while blacks were mentally capable yet morally feeble.[35] Because the white race, according to Armstrong, was morally strong precisely because of its unique historical experiences, it seemed logical that whites should preside over the ex-slaves' gradual transition into civilized life.

The Hampton-Tuskegee model taught students that the position of their race was not the result of oppression but of the natural process of cultural evolution. The model taught that people should accept the natural state of things. Further, blacks who declined to accept it were "foolish." The point of the Hampton model was that it deliberately taught prospective black leaders, including Attwell, economic values that were not progressive and productive for the economic interests of black citizens.

There was much criticism of the Hampton-Tuskegee model, particularly from some blacks. A significant number of Hampton's students criticized the school's industrial program because, from the students' vantage point, the trade instruction was elementary and limited. Black criticism of Hampton received national attention in the late 1870s when two black writers characterized the Hampton program as an educational experience that sought to affirm the legitimacy of black subordination. After attending an 1876 commencement, one writer, appalled by Hampton's pattern of race relations, reported:

> On Commencement Day May 18th, visitors were present, both white and colored, but not one of the latter was to be seen on the splendid platform of Virginia Hall. The rudest and most ignorant white men and women were politely conducted to the platform; respectable and intelligent colored ladies and gentlemen were shown lower seats where they could neither see nor hear the exercises of the day with any pleasure. To speak in general the colored people and students are made to feel that they must forever remain inferior to their white brethren no matter what their attainments may be.[36]

The development of the recreation and leisure participation and interest of blacks in conjunction with the Hampton-Tuskegee model was problematic. Under this model blacks were told to keep doing what they had been doing and not to seek a broad-based or refined approach to recreation and leisure.

Many blacks viewed Booker T. Washington as a traitor and collaborator.[37] Even one of Washington's biographers has been critical of his philosophy. His philosophy was admired by whites because he transcended his experience of victimization without any trace of psychological debilitation or bitterness toward whites.

The most serious opposition to Booker T. Washington and the Hampton-Tuskegee model came from W.E.B. Du Bois. Washington and Du Bois were involved in some of the most important debates in American history. Each represented contrasting strategies for black political protest and self-help. In retrospect, the civil rights movement followed the course outlined by Du Bois over that of Washington; and it is fairly obvious that, for many mainstream black civil rights activists, Booker T. Washington and his views were an embarrassment.

Washington and Du Bois had different backgrounds and experiences which affected their philosophies. Washington was born a southern slave and had to overcome significant obstacles to become one of America's leading black educators, orators, and institution builders. Du Bois was born a free man in the North at about the same time that Washington was founding the Tuskegee Institute. Du Bois was a very educated man who attended schools in both Europe and the United States. He was the first black to receive a postgraduate degree from Harvard University in 1895. To Du Bois and his followers, Washington's approach appeared accommodationist. He was portrayed as the original "Uncle Tom," willing to settle for crumbs from the white man's table rather than fight for the equal rights due to all free men. Du Bois, on the other hand, advocated a more militant approach which encouraged fighting for every right that belonged to all Americans.

The Hampton-Tuskegee model was supported by a number of prominent Americans including Ulysses S. Grant, Rutherford B. Hayes, James Garfield, Theodore Roosevelt, William Taft, and Woodrow Wilson. Consequently, Attwell, after studying under this model, liked to quote Roosevelt by stating, "America will not be a good place for any of us to live in unless it is a good place for all of us to live in."

Though adhering to much of the Hampton-Tuskegee philosophy, Attwell was well-suited to serve as a liaison between the white and black communities, considering the political climate of the times. With America in a period of incrementalism, the National Recreation Association wanted a black representative who would not be too confrontational when it attempted to expand recreation and leisure opportunities for black citizens.

However, while operating in this very conservative period, Attwell made progress toward the attainment of better recreation and leisure opportunities for blacks. In 1919 when he began working for the National Recreation Association, few U.S cities were providing appropriate recreation programs for blacks. The first significant recreational programming for blacks began in centers established for military personnel by the War Camp Community Service. Attwell's first assignment was to transform these centers into permanent community recreation centers. In the first nine years after Attwell joined the association's staff, the number of cities reporting black recreation leaders identified in the *Recreation Yearbook* increased from 28 to 103, while the actual number of black recreation leaders rose from 35 to over 400.[38] Attwell was wise to point out during the 1928 national Conference of Social Work that although progress was being made,

> Millions of colored children and adults of this racial group representing one tenth of our population have never felt the thrill of discovering a playground within their neighborhood; thousands more have not yet received the tremendous value of leisure-time guidance or trained leadership in play or recreational activities. The development of recreation for Negroes is in the "covered wagon" stage.

Notes/References

1. Charles S. Johnson. 1930. *The Negro in American Civilization: A Study of Negro Life and Race Relations in the Light of Social Research*. New York: Henry Holt and Company, 301.

2. George E. Haynes. 1918. Negro New Comers in Detroit: A Challenge to Christian Statesmanship; A Preliminary Survey, By Home Missions Council

3. Guzman, 192.

4. *Duke Ellington's Washington: A Profile of Washington's Black Community*. 2000. Produced and reported by Hedrick Smith, produced and directed by Stanley Nelson. Premiered February 7 on PBS.

5. W. E. B. DuBois. 1899/1999. *The Philadelphia Negro: A Social Study*. Philadelphia: University of Pennsylvania Press, 469.

6. *Duke Ellington's Washington*.

7. Jessie P. Guzman, ed. 1952. *1952 Negro Yearbook*. New York: Wm. H. Wise & Co., 191.

8. DuBois, 467.

9. Ibid., 470.

10. Carter G. Woodson. 1921. *The History of the Negro Church*. Washington, DC: Associated Press, 267–68.

11. Gunnar Myrdal. 1971. The Negro church in the Negro community. In *The Black Church in America*. Hart Nelsen, Raytha Yokely, and Anne Nelsen, eds. New York: Basic Books, 82–90.

12. Benjamin E. Mays and J. W. Nicholson. 1969. *The Negro's Church*. New York: Negro Universities Press, 122–23.

13. W. E. B. DuBois. 1971. The function of the church. In *The Black Church in America*. Hart Nelsen, Raytha Yokely, and Anne Nelsen, eds. New York: Basic Books, 77–81.

14. G. Myrdal. 1944. *An American Dilemma: The Negro Problem and Modern Democracy*, vol. 2. New York: Harper & Brothers, 984.

15. D. Lewis. 1981. *When Harlem Was in Vogue*. New York: Alfred A. Knopf, 88–118.

16. Mel Watkins. 1994. *On the Real Side: Laughing, Lying, and Signifying— The Underground Tradition of African-American Humor That Transformed American Culture, from Slavery to Richard Pryor*. New York: Simon & Schuster, 204.

17. Molefi Kete Asante and Mark Mattson. 1992. *Historical and Cultural Atlas of African Americans*. New York: Macmillan Publishing, 113–15.

18. T. S. Suttle. 1916. Recreation for Negroes in Memphis. *The Playground* 9, no. 12 (March): 441.

19. Pilz, J. J. 1985. The beginnings of organized play for black Americans: E.T. Attwell and the PRAA. *Journal of Negro History* 70, no. 3/4 (Summer-Autumn): 60.

20. Poster from National Recreation and Parks Association. 1998. 100 Years of Parks and Recreation. *Parks and Recreation*: 1898–1998.

21. Thomas Parker. 1926. Recreation for colored citizens. The Playground 19, no. 12 (March): 651.

22. Pilz, 63.

23. Ruth Russell. 1986. *Leadership in Recreation*. St. Louis, MO: Times Mirror/Mosby College Publishing, 277.

24. Christopher Edginton, Debra Jordan, Donald DeGraaf, and Debra Edginton. 1996. *Leisure and Life Satisfaction: Foundational Perspectives*. Madison, WI, and Dubuque, IA: Brown and Benchmark, 332.

25. Russell, 5–10.

26. Thomas J. Woofter. 1928. *Negro Problems in Cities*. College Park, MD: McGrath Publishing Company. Attwell wrote this in the May 1923 issue of *Opportunity*.

27. Ernest Ten Eyck Attwell. 1921. Playgrounds for colored America. *The Playground* 15, no. 1 (April): 85–86.

28. G. D. Butler. 1965. *Pioneers in Public Recreation*. Minneapolis, MN: Burgess Publishing Company, 160–67.

29. Ibid.

30. Ernest Ten Eyck Attwell. 1949. *Recreation* 43, no. 6 (September): 307.

31. Attwell (1921): 86.

32. Playground and Recreation Association of America. 1927. Maintaining community service. Bulletin no. 91.

33. Pilz, 60.

34. James D. Anderson. 1988. *The Education of Blacks in the South, 1860–1935*. Chapel Hill, NC: University of North Carolina Press, 36.

35. Anderson, 61–62.

36. Ibid., 63.

37. Dinesh D'Sousa. 1995. *The End of Racism: Principles for a Multicultural Society*. New York: Free Press, 184.

38. Butler, 161.

PART THREE

Chapter 10

AFTER SEPARATE-BUT-EQUAL

This section offers insight and perspective on contemporary black recreation through a brief discussion of selected events affecting this recreation experience. Specifically, attention is given to some significant occurrences, recreational and otherwise, affecting blacks and their recreation and leisure since 1954. Then black recreation opportunity and participation in the 1960s through the 1980s will be briefly addressed, followed by a discussion of the contributions of the Ethnic Minority Society of the National Recreation and Park Association to black recreation in America. Finally, a brief inquiry touches on black recreation in the 1990s and the start of the twenty-first century.

The Impact of Civil Rights Legislation

Nineteen fifty-four was a benchmark year for America, the year when federal law mandated equality between the races by eliminating the separate-but-equal doctrine. In 1954 with the *Brown v. Board of Education* decision, America forged a new mode of thought, calling for impartiality in all public accommodations including land acquisition, facilities, and leadership. Not until 1954 and *Brown* did the Supreme Court officially reverse the separate-but-equal law of the land. For the first time, at least theoretically, there could be true racial equality. However, blacks were to learn that there are two kinds of segregation: *de jure*, mandated by law, and *de facto*, existing in reality.

The impact of segregation came to the forefront in the area of "education access and opportunity." In *Brown* the Supreme Court declared that racial segregation in public schools violated the U.S. Constitution. Emotions ran high as Americans wrestled with this issue. The insensitivity of the separate-but-equal doctrine was dramatized by a seven-year-old child named Linda Brown. In 1950 Linda and her parents moved to an integrated neighborhood in Topeka, Kansas. Linda's parents tried to enroll her in the all-white public school only four blocks away. Under the separate-but-equal law, Linda was denied enrollment and told she would have to leave her white and Mexican-American playmates and take a bus almost two miles to the "Negro" school.

The lead attorney for the plaintiffs was Thurgood Marshall, a black civil-rights lawyer who would go on to become the first black Supreme Court Justice. He was an exceptional attorney. Throughout the trial he and other supporting attorneys shed light on a number of racial inequalities. For example, most whites and blacks were unaware of the far-reaching effects of America's segregation laws that included: prohibiting textbooks used by whites and blacks to be stored together or interchanged; requiring separate phone booths for blacks; requiring separate seating at circuses; requiring separation in hospitals; prohibiting interracial fraternal organizations; penalizing anyone who circulated printed material advocating social equality or intermarriage between blacks and whites; forbidding the chaining together of white and black chain-gang prisoners; and requiring white nurses for white patients and black nurses for black patients.[1] These realities demonstrated the depth of the separate-but-equal legislation.

Although the plaintiffs lost early court rulings, the case was eventually appealed to the Supreme Court where Marshall and his team presented an exceptional case. Subsequently, Chief Justice Earl Warren read the court's decision:

In approaching this problem, we cannot turn the clock back to . . . 1896 when *Plessy v. Ferguson* was written. We must consider public education in the light of its full development and its present place in American life throughout the Nation. Only in this way can it be determined if segregation in public schools deprives these plaintiffs of the equal protection of the laws.

Today, education is perhaps the most important function of state and local governments. Compulsory school attendance laws and the great expenditures for education both demonstrate our recognition of the importance of education to our democratic society. It is required in the performance of our most basic public responsibilities, even service in the armed forces. It is the very foundation of good citizenship.

We come then to the question presented: Does segregation of children in public schools solely on the basis of race, even though the physical facilities and other "tangible" factors may be equal, deprive the children of the minority group of equal educational opportunities? We believe that it does.

. . . To separate them from others of similar age and qualifications solely because of their race generates a feeling of inferiority as to their status in the community that may affect their hearts and minds in a way unlikely ever to be undone. The effect of this separation on their educational opportunities was well stated by a finding in the Kansas case by a court which nevertheless felt compelled to rule against the Negro plaintiffs:

> Segregation of white and colored children in public schools has a detrimental effect upon the colored children. The impact is greater when it has the sanction of the law; for the policy of separating the races is usually interpreted as denoting the inferiority of the Negro group. A sense of inferiority affects the motivation of a child to learn. Segregation with the sanction of law, therefore, has a tendency to [retard] the educational and mental development of Negro children and to deprive them of some of the benefits they would receive in a racial[ly] integrated school system.

Whatever may have been the extent of psychological knowledge at the time of *Plessy v. Ferguson*, this finding is amply supported by modern authority. Any language in *Plessy v. Ferguson* contrary to this finding is rejected.

We conclude that in the field of public education the doctrine of "separate but equal" has no place. Separate educational facilities are inherently unequal. Therefore, we hold that the plaintiffs and others similarly situated for whom the actions have been brought are, by reason of the segregation complained of, deprived of the equal protection of the laws guaranteed by the Fourteenth Amendment.[2] (Reprinted with permission. Carl T. Rowan, 1993. *Dream Makers, Dream Breakers: The World of Justice Thurgood Marshall*. Boston: Little, Brown and Company, 216–17).

The Court's voice was loud and clear: "*No more segregation.*" Segregation was a deterrent to racial equality. Nonetheless, passage of laws alone could not guarantee inclusion and integration. Even after *Brown*, the struggle for equality continued. About one year after the *Brown* decision, the struggle for equal civil rights took a significant turn with the help of a determined middle-aged black woman in Montgomery, Alabama, whose feet were aching after an exhausting day's work. Rosa Parks, whose name will be forever etched in the racial memory of America, was coming home from work on December 1, 1955, and couldn't find a seat in the back of the bus where blacks were supposed to sit. Instead, she took a seat near the middle to rest and relax. The bus eventually filled with white passengers and Rosa was told to move to the back of the bus. She refused because there were no seats in back where the other blacks were seated, and she was arrested for violating the city's transportation laws. Some four days later, the Reverend Martin Luther King Jr. led a boycott of public transportation by blacks in Montgomery. For over a year blacks boycotted and walked, rode bicycles, drove, or got rides around the city rather than use the buses. Eventually, in 1956 the Parks case was tried before the Supreme Court which ruled in favor of the black boycotters, declaring that blacks could take any seat they wanted on municipal buses. Although the outcome was positive for blacks as well as whites, the decision was a difficult one for America to digest.

Ten years after *Brown*, the nation affirmed its commitment to equality for all citizens with the enactment of the Civil Rights Act of 1964, one of America's most influential pieces of civil rights legislation, one which marked the beginning of a new era in American life. This act made it unlawful to discriminate on the basis of race, color, religion, or national origin in educational institutions, workplaces, and public facilities. The enactment of this legislation was significant and progressive for a nation with blatant discriminatory attitudes and practices. Yet even after the passage of the Civil Rights Act and the elimination of separate-but-equal, African Americans continued to run into a series of barriers to full participation in public accommodations, including recreation and leisure.

Black Recreation from 1954 through the 1980s

Since 1954 one of the primary challenges for the recreation profession has been to broaden the participation of those who are underrepresented in recreation opportunity. This challenge brings with it the realization that recreation participation enhances quality of life, producing a happier and more contented society. Americans currently spend heavily on recreation—more than $300 billion annually—so the recreation profession is wise to be as inclusive as possible and to welcome and attract the broadest range of participants. The desire to do this began in earnest in the mid-1950s.

Incrementally, after the separate-but-equal period, whites began to take a more active interest in recreation and its benefits to all. There was growing realization and acknowledgment that engagement in recreation and leisure was beneficial for everyone, including blacks. This brought an increased awareness of the need for equal rights in America.

However, acknowledgment of the benefits of recreation for all was not enough to ensure equal opportunity. More proof was needed of the consequences of inequality. Even discussions and reports on the effects of recreation and quality of life in America— for example, crime reduction and improvement in the health of all citizens—were slow to increase recreation opportunity for blacks in America. They confronted obstacles at every turn.

Regardless of the elimination of the separate-but-equal doctrine it was not uncommon to visit both sides of the tracks (referring to the old practice of blacks and whites living separated by railroad tracks) and see very different communities. Most black neighborhoods were very much in need of repair compared to white neighborhoods in the same cities. In addition to noteworthy housing and neighborhood differences, it was common to find radically different recreation facilities and equipment, including parks and playgrounds, in the same municipality. Somehow—pessimists might say coincidentally—blacks always received the inferior facilities, programming, leadership, and equipment. As a young boy growing up in the South in the late 1950s and 1960s, I distinctly remember a city with a white YMCA and YWCA and a black YMCA and YWCA. The white Ys definitely looked better—at least from the outside, and few if any blacks ever entered the white facilities. The white YMCA building was newer, larger, better-maintained, and even the sidewalks outside were well-kept. Peering through its windows, I saw the finest recreation and fitness equipment. On the other hand, the black Y was in need of repair. It was much smaller, had no swimming pool, and its equipment was rarely what one would consider top quality. Not until much later, during the late '60s and early '70s, did YMCAs and YWCAs throughout America (organizations that supposedly emphasized world fellowship and interracial understanding) begin to provide roughly equal facilities, equipment, and leadership for whites and blacks. As evidenced by this example, black communities received far less for recreation (land, leadership, and facilities) than their white counterparts, and this inequality was not due to the luck of the draw.

Federal Agency Involvement: The PWA

As discussed in previous sections, blacks resorted to a number of strategies to improve their recreation opportunity. This push for equal recreational services was later aided by the federal government through the provision of additional funding for services and facilities in black communities. Actually, the government's involvement began prior to 1954. During the Depression federal agencies rather than local municipalities provided more (although only slightly) of the basic rights of blacks in recreation. Title II of the National Industrial Recovery Act provided for the establishment of a Public Works Administration (PWA) with an appropriation of $3.3 billion to finance a large public works program.[3] One of the major objectives of the PWA was to supplement the stimulation of economic recovery. Realizing that the construction of public works offered significant temptations for favoritism and corruption, President Franklin D. Roosevelt required the spending to be scrutinized with care. The PWA was very slow in getting under way. It spent only $110 million of the $3.3 billion that it was allocated in the first six months of its existence.

The PWA and later the Works Progress Administration (WPA) had a dual purpose: the building of useful public projects and the provision of employment for those in need. Both these objectives stood to benefit blacks in their recreation opportunities. As an organization, the PWA was more conscientious about special needs of the poor than any other industrial or agricultural agency established in 1933.[4] Many blacks were employed through the PWA, but its employment policies were not without problems, and there was continued discrimination against blacks throughout the United States.

The second purpose of the PWA, the construction of government-subsidized facilities, was also beneficial for blacks. The most obvious benefit was the construction of low-rent housing.[5] Blacks benefited because some of the government projects included the renovation or building of additional public parks, recreation facilities, and swimming pools.

By providing these additional facilities, the WPA demonstrated interest and involvement in often neglected recreation facilities. For example, in 1937 the WPA constructed 440 municipal swimming pools, 123 golf courses, 1,500 athletic fields, and 3,500 tennis courts in the South.[6] Although whites received far more, blacks did get some of the benefits of additional recreational facilities in their communities. It was at the federal level (as it often is today) and not at the local level that the change was initiated. Through such efforts federal agencies succeeded in providing more recreational facility availability to black communities.

The NRPA and the Ethnic Minority Society

It was not until the civil unrest of the 1960s that the recreation profession and society in general attempted to understand the importance of recreation in the lives of all citizens, not just whites.

Especially in the larger cities where much social unrest occurred—some of it over the use of recreation facilities—serious attention was paid. During the civil rights era, America's social engineers sought ways to bring whites and blacks together. Instead of seeking this connection in the workplace, churches, hotels, and restaurants, many focused on the recreation establishment.

In retrospect, recreation was a logical place to initiate better race relations because recreation is more likely to be voluntary. In the workplace individuals must work together, in churches they must worship together, in restaurants they generally eat in the same environment, and in hotels they stay in rooms previously occupied by others. Blacks and whites might not be willing to pray together, eat together, learn together—and certainly not to sleep together!—but they might succeed at playing together.

Since recreation was voluntary in nature, it was judged by many to be a good first bridge for the races to cross toward racial harmony. In the 1960s and 1970s, recreation seemed an area for compromise, especially in urban areas. Maybe at play people would and could address inequalities, promote unity, and lessen the gap between blacks and whites in America. Perhaps in recreation there would be less resistance to integration from both whites and blacks.

To more fully understand the public and private advancement of blacks in recreation, consider a group of professionals who had a definitive influence on black recreation, the founders of the Playground Association of America (PAA). In 1906 a small group of dedicated professionals met at the White House in Washington, D.C., "to establish some effective means of connecting their individual efforts and concerns and communicating information gained from their experiences in different cities."[7] Some of them became prominent in the recreation and leisure field—Joseph Lee, Henry Curtis, Jane Addams, and Luther Gulick. Their meeting ended with the formation of the first professional recreation organization, the PAA. In 1965, through the growth and merger of other, more recently-formed professional recreation organizations, the National Recreation and Park Association (NRPA) was formed.

The NRPA is an independent nonprofit organization whose goals include the development and promotion of the recreation and parks movement, and the conservation of natural and human resources in the United States. A number of separate branches carry out the work and unite the special interests of NRPA members. One of these special interest groups is the Ethnic Minority Society (EMS).

Prior to the formal establishment of the EMS, during the 1969 National Recreation and Park Congress, a small group of black professionals, including Ira Hutchinson, Nate Washington, and Pearl Vaughn established the Black Caucus. The Black Caucus was probably the first formally organized group of blacks to work in unison within the NRPA. The primary reason for the development of the caucus was the increasing pressure by persons of color for more inclusion in America's recreation system. The NRPA was having limited success in this area. Essentially, the Black Caucus was formed out of frustration with the NRPA, which was not appropriately addressing black recreation needs and interests.

In 1971 the Black Caucus matriculated into the Ethnic Minority Society (EMS) of the NRPA. The EMS is comprised primarily of persons of color in the NRPA. Founding members of the EMS included Thelma Stewart, Ben Anderson, Yvonne Washington, and Irving Gregory, among others.[8] The developmental timing of the EMS was important. From the middle 1960s through the 1970s America was in turmoil. Relations between blacks and whites were tense and tenuous. Blacks were demanding equal rights and privileges, but many whites were reluctant to relinquish their privileged status.

The major events of the time reflected race relations of the period. In 1964 Dr. Martin Luther King won the Nobel Prize for Peace, and later the same year America passed the monumental Civil Rights Act of 1964. The very next year Malcolm X, a powerfully outspoken opponent of the treatment of black Americans, was assassinated in Harlem, New York. In 1966 Huey Newton and Bobby Seale founded the militant Black Panther Party in Oakland, California. That same year, Stokely Carmichael was elected head of the Student Nonviolent Coordinating Committee. These events clearly indicate the delicate nature of race relations at that time.

The period was also marked by President Lyndon Johnson's appointment of Thurgood Marshall to the Supreme Court in 1967. Marshall was the first black person to hold such high office. The next year, however, King was assassinated in Memphis, Tennessee, an event that sent America reeling in confusion and disbelief. In the midst of this crisis, numerous national organizations formed coalitions to protect and ensure the rights of their black members. For example, in 1972 the National Black Political Convention had its inaugural meeting in Gary, Indiana.

Minority (particularly black) recreation professionals likewise established a proactive black agenda through the formation of the EMS. Importantly, the EMS was not welcomed with joy by many NRPA members. The NRPA initially provided little, if any, support for the emerging organization whose goals included more minority involvement in NRPA social activity and development of programs unique to urban populations. In protest, EMS went to the then-president of the NRPA Dwight Reddick and asked for more support in meeting their goals. Initially, Reddick was not sympathetic, so the EMS used such intimidation tactics as vowing to identify the NRPA as racist unless it acceded to EMS's requests. Eventually, the NRPA weakened and began to provide more support to the EMS which has since evolved into an important constituency within the NPRA.

Notes/References

1. Carl Rowan. 1993. *Dream Makers, Dream Breakers: The World of Justice Thurgood Marshall*. Boston: Little, Brown and Company.

2. Ibid., 216–17.

3. Raymond Wolters. 1970. *Negroes and the Great Depression: The Problem of Recovery*. Westport, CT: Greenwood Publishing, 193.

4. Wolters, 196.

5. Ibid., 198.

6. John S. Ezell. 1975. *The South Since 1865*, 2nd ed. New York: Macmillan Publishing, 339.

7. Ruth Russell. 1996. *Pastimes: The Context of Contemporary Leisure*. Glenview, IL: Brown and Benchmark, 276.

8. Information obtained from personal interviews with EMS members, including Ben Anderson and Yvonne Washington, at the 1999 NRPA Congress in Nashville, Tennessee.

Chapter 11

THE BLACK RECREATION EXPERIENCE IN THE 1990s AND INTO THE TWENTY-FIRST CENTURY

The Black Recreation Experience

Gunnar Myrdal, who chronicled one of the first widely accepted comprehensive analyses of African-American life believed that Americans would make great racial strides in bringing about equality between the races. Even during the troubled late 1960s Myrdal retained his optimistic outlook.[1] Obviously, Myrdal did not correctly analyze the data that led him to this conclusion. It is apparent that, as we move into this new millennium, racial problems still permeate America. In fact, many argue that the race problem remains one of the nation's deepest dilemmas.

Leisure is now the largest category of time in a person's day; the free time of Americans has grown enormously since the early 1900s.[2] Many scholars are investigating this increased leisure, and it is apparent that Americans desire even *more* free time. Fortunately, as we forge into the 2000s, it is evident that the recreation profession and its professionals are devoting more attention to issues of race and to the ways blacks and other minority groups use their leisure time. The *Therapeutic Recreation Journal*, the leading publisher of therapeutic recreation research has published more articles addressing race and ethnicity. In addition, in November 1998 the *Journal of Leisure Research* devoted an entire volume to race and ethnicity issues in the profession. If one carefully observes the specific agendas and presentations at noteworthy national, regional, and local recreation and leisure conferences, it is clear that at least superficial attention is being directed toward race and recreation. In the future, it is likely that more recreation publications will devote more genuine attention to race and its impact on the profession.

In 1994 the National Recreation and Park Association released an important study providing more evidence that municipal recreation helps prevent many serious social problems, including juvenile delinquency. The report, "Beyond Fun and Games: Emerging Roles of Public Recreation," concluded that quality recreation helps reduce crime, improves health and quality of life, and creates safer communities.[3] Richard Kraus, a leading professor of leisure from Temple University, agrees on the linkage between recreation and delinquency, and also believes that recreation can be a means of overcoming hostility and tension in many urban communities.

Meanwhile, the federal government now recognizes the importance of gaining reliable information on all of its citizens, including blacks, and subsidizes such research. For example, Myron Floyd of Texas A & M University, one of the nation's research leaders on race and recreation, and Kimberly Shinew of the University of Illinois received a grant from the USDA Forest Service to conduct a study of the relationship of race, gender, and social class in urban parks and forests. Floyd and Shinew are attempting to identify factors related to park use patterns among blacks and whites in the Chicago metropolitan area. This type of research, although longitudinal in nature, is useful because it assists policymakers in understanding the needs, constraints, and preferences of both black and white urban park users.

Along with the work of Floyd and Shinew, one of the more interesting analyses of modern recreation participation by Americans comes from the Recreation Roundtable. The Recreation Roundtable is a Washington, D.C.-based group created to contemplate some of the larger questions regarding outdoor recreation participation in America. The Roundtable, created by the nonprofit American Recreation Coalition, consists of some of industry's high level executives who have business interests in Americans who spend billions of dollars on outdoor recreation. The Roundtable uses a number of quality indicators to measure recreation in America, including perceived opportunity for, participation in, and satisfaction with outdoor physical activities. These indicators calibrate the extent to which Americans have physical access to activities and the amount of time and money necessary to take advantage of them. Other indicators measure which activities are engaged in and whether individuals plan to increase or decrease their involvement in the next year. Finally, the Roundtable seeks to calculate individual happiness with the value and quality of specific forms of outdoor recreation participation.

Using 1994 as a milestone, the Roundtable found that the quality indicators had risen from the previous year, implying that Americans were more involved and increasingly satisfied with their outdoor recreation. Most Americans indicated that lack of time was the greatest constraint on their recreation participation, followed by cost and lack of interest. Interestingly, most Americans reject the idea that outdoor recreation activities are only for the wealthy. In fact, the Roundtable concluded that recreation in America is quite egalitarian. However, its remaining data contradicted this conclusion. For example, it found that participation was significantly greater among those with more education and those with higher incomes. Other findings showed that residents of large urban areas and blacks (who happen to be more numerous in many urban areas) had lower levels of participation and opportunity. Finally, the Roundtable's findings indicated that the dominant reason for lower than average participation was fear of crime.

More recent findings from the Roundtable are even more revealing. The 1997 report indicates that among some groups— including working women, young single persons, and blacks— recreation participation was declining. The report's results measured "real" and "perceived" recreation opportunities and satisfaction with outdoor recreation, and they showed a sharp decline in the indicators. The Recreation Quality Index (RQI) for working women was 110 in 1997, down from 122 in 1996. For African Americans, the RQI dropped from 89 in 1996 to 76 in 1997; for single persons under 45, the RQI fell to 104 in 1997 from 117 in 1996.

Much current research regarding blacks in recreation seeks answers to the ethnicity/marginality issues presented earlier. One of the more interesting studies of this type was reported by Stephen Philipp of the University of West Florida. Philipp investigated differences between middle-class blacks and whites in their perceptions of how welcome blacks were in selected leisure activities. [4] This study presented a number of interesting discoveries:

(a) Middle-class blacks and whites tended to agree about where blacks would and would not be welcome.
(b) Middle-class blacks feel much *less* welcome in most leisure activities than middle-class whites believe.
(c) When thinking of themselves as parents, blacks and whites agree on the activities that are important for children; yet significantly more whites than blacks rated many additional activities as very important for their children.

Philipp's study may shed light on the most current status of blacks in recreation in America. It seems that racial groups share both similarities and differences in recreation experiences and in their perceptions of those experiences. As economically similar yet racially different individuals, blacks and whites may value certain of the same activities, but blacks may not so frequently engage in such activities, thus sending negative messages to their black children. The engagement of blacks depends heavily on the perceptions of how they are welcomed by whites.

This in itself would support the ethnicity hypothesis presented early in this book. Essentially, as blacks feel less welcome in certain activities, they engage instead in activities that many other blacks engage in. Over time, these activities may become so ingrained in the black psyche that they are racially and culturally stabilized. This supports the ethnicity theory. In retrospect, Philipp's notion of racial discrimination and its impact on recreation participation may be more relevant to black and white recreation participation and involvement than is currently realized.[5]

Quality of Life and
Black Recreation Participation

Quality of life and its relationship to blacks and their recreation is as important as the issues of marginality and ethnicity. Does recreation impact quality of life? Has recreation improved quality of life for blacks? Has recreation affected quality of life for blacks to the same degree that it has for whites? Is race a significant determinant of quality of life for blacks? Answering these questions requires cautious and continuous incremental methodology and analysis.

There is evidence to suggest that blacks score consistently lower than whites on measures of psychological well-being.[6] As psychological well-being is indicative of quality of life, this suggests that race issues continue to pervade the overall well-being of blacks. Many scholars have attempted to expand the discussion so as to discover whether the race issue is increasing or decreasing as a factor in life satisfaction and quality of life. Whether the significance of race is increasing or decreasing may be less salient than whether race continues to determine the quality of life and well-being of African Americans.

To be sure, recreation and leisure are important to overall individual quality of life. The recreation literature is filled with acknowledgments of this reality. The quality-of-life approach to recreation and leisure has been used since the 1950s. This approach "sees recreation as an experience that contributes to human development and to community well-being in various ways: improving physical and mental health, enriching cultural life, reducing antisocial uses of leisure, and strengthening community ties."[7] The quality-of-life approach emphasizes concepts such as self-choice, freedom, and pleasure as the most meaningful benefits of recreation and leisure. Using the quality-of-life framework, recreation should be engaged in for its own sake, because of the value it brings to the individual. If blacks, both children and adults, do not engage in recreation because of fear, discomfort in the environment, lack of access, or absence of opportunity, the resulting long-term consequences may be detrimental to all of America. For example, if the fear of crime is a major deterrent to recreation participation, America may pay the price in coming generations.

A lack of opportunity ultimately results in a lack of creativity, and lack of creativity is stifling to the individual. Given the continued societal imbalance between black and white Americans, blacks may continue to feel like lesser, weaker, and unwanted citizens. Those who feel society treats them as inferior may react in ways that appear defensive and aggressive, even in disruptive and potentially anti-social behavior.

One of the most explored areas of recreation for blacks is the area of children and adolescents. Quite possibly it is prudent to direct most attention to the youth. Studies show that adults who indicate that recreation was very important to them when they grew up are likely to continue involvement and participation in this recreation. [8] Significantly, those who continue to participate in recreational and leisure activities in adulthood are more satisfied with virtually all aspects of their lives.

Much of the theoretical literature focusing on leisure and personality development indicates that leisure plays an important role in adolescent development.[9] Underlying this notion is the idea that recreation and leisure activities provide opportunities for adolescents to find acceptance among their peers and to understand how leisure impacts adulthood.[10] However most research on the affects of leisure on youth has been conducted primarily with white youth. Add the potential race factor to the complexities of adolescent development and it is clear that the same findings may not be applicable to black and other minority youth. Hence, more empirical research needs to be done on the impact of race on the recreation of children and adolescents. This is especially important because adolescent recreation and leisure preferences are generally considered important to adult leisure behavior.

Black youths and adolescents sometimes present particularly troublesome problems for the recreation professional. Many in the recreation profession attest that much traditional recreation programming does not interest and/or meet the needs of black adolescents. Yet, there is a construct in America that asserts that effective recreation programming can have a positive impact on youth. This is particularly true of minority or urban youth in terms of crime prevention. Numerous professional attempts have been made to address the problem. "Midnight" or late-evening basketball was developed to provide alternative recreation and leisure activity for youngsters. These programs have had positive results in some locales and very little impact in others. Such constructive activity in the late-evening and early morning hours, the time when much delinquent activity occurs, was thought to be a way of keeping youths off the streets and engaged in recreation, thus reducing juvenile crime.

Some early studies on the play of black and white children are also interesting and provide additional insight. One of the earliest studies compared the play activities of white and black school-children and found that black children participated more actively than white children in social forms of play.[11] Many prevailing attitudes and stereotypical ideas about blacks and their play can be attributed to early scholars in the profession. These writers studied the play of blacks and drew conclusions about why blacks play and recreate as they do. Proclaiming blacks to be of inferior academic intelligence, Harvey Lehma and Paul Witty [12] postulated that black children played "school" more than white children as a symbolic way of assimilating a type of activity they were academically or socially unable to engage in in reality.

Past inquiry on adolescent recreation and leisure behavior has largely ignored race as a variable, even though race has been the single most important factor influencing employment, housing, and education in the United States.[13] It is reasonable to assume that race is also a significant factor in recreation. Steven Philipp provides revealing data in his study "Race and Gender Differences in Adolescent Peer Group Approval of Leisure Activities".[14] Although limited in the number of study participants, Philipp provides some much needed insight on the significance of race and gender. His analysis found that race was a more important variable than gender in peer group approval of leisure activities.

Conclusion

Despite the 1964 Civil Rights Act, racial discrimination persists, particularly against blacks. All one has to do is read newspapers or watch current newscasts to realize the impact of modern racial discrimination and prejudice. There is also a constant underrepresentation of blacks in many areas of life, including employment, higher education, and recreation and leisure. Such inequalities are probably attributable to intentional and unintentional racial discrimination. As we move into a new century, it may be optimistic yet entirely appropriate to suggest that most racism is institutional. In 1978 Joe and Clairece Feagin, in their book *Discrimination American Style: Institutional Racism and Sexism* coined the phrase "institutional racism" to describe this perspective. The Feagins' proposition is that racism has moved from old-fashioned, personalized discrimination against minorities toward institutionalized discrimination in the employment arena.[15] The Feagins assert that the modern problem of racism and discrimination arises from the perspective from which one views the issue.

After more than a century, the injustices of slavery and segregation should be fairly well erased from the memories of both white and black Americans. That is not the case. Over time the physical scars of slavery have faded, but many blacks express concern that even four hundred years after the first African was brought to the United States, the effects of that degrading experience are still felt. Both whites and blacks have harbored protracted emotional distress caused by the mistreatment of blacks during slavery and in the years of separate-but-equal. Blacks, as the victims, have deeper wounds to heal.

As mentioned early in this book, specific theories have been developed to help explain differences in recreation and leisure participation between whites and blacks. In addition to the theories identified early in the book to account for such differences in play, recreation, and leisure interest, participation, and involvement, another theory may apply: the racial consciousness theory. The racial consciousness theory asserts that the degree to which a person is racially conscious—regardless of his/her socioeconomic status, race, or opportunity afforded—can account for recreation and leisure differences and preferences. The basis of this theory is that those blacks who are most racially conscious recognize the subjugation of black people and poignantly articulate the extent to which this subjugation is rooted simultaneously in racial and economic equalities. There is a sense of collective struggle for blacks in this model, and the struggle continues.

Notes/References

1. David W. Southern. 1987. *Gunnar Myrdal and Black-White Relations: The Use and Abuse of an American Dilemma, 1944–1969.* Baton Rouge: Louisiana State University Press, 308.

2. Michael Leitner and Sara Leitner. 1996. *Leisure Enhancement,* 2nd ed. New York: Haworth Press, 51.

3. Richard Kraus. 1997. *Recreation and Leisure in Modern Society,* 5th ed. Menlo Park, CA: Addison Wesley Longman, 136.

4. Stephen Philipp. 1999. Are we welcome? African-American acceptance in leisure activities and the importance given to children's leisure. *Journal of Leisure Research* 31 (4): 385–403.

5. Stephen Philipp. 1995. Race and leisure constraints. *Journal of Leisure Research* 17: 109–120.; Philipp (1999), 385–403.

6. M. Thomas and M. Hughes. 1986. The continuing significance of race: A study of race, class, and quality of life in America, 1972–1985. *American Sociological Review* 51: 830–41.

7. Kraus, 382.

8. Neil H. Cheek and W. Burch. 1976. *The Social Organization of Leisure in Human Society.* New York: Harper & Row; Mihaly Csikszentmihalyi, Reed Larson, and S. Prescott. 1977. The ecology of adolescent activity and experience. *Journal of Youth and Adolescence* 6: 281–94.; Seppo Iso-Ahola. 1980. *The Social Psychology of Leisure and Recreation.* Dubuque, IA: Brown Publishers.

9. S. Shaw, D. Kleiber, and L. Cadwell. 1995. Leisure and identity formation in male and female adolescents: A preliminary examination. *Journal of Leisure Research* 27: 245–63.

10. John Kelly. 1990. *Leisure.* Englewood Cliffs, NJ: Prentice Hall, 50–79.

11. Harry C. Lehman and P. Witty. 1927. *The Psychology of Play Activities.* New York: A. S. Barnes.

12. Ibid., 161.

13. Gerald D. Jaynes and Robin M. Williams. 1989 *A Common Destiny: Blacks and American Society.* Washington, DC: National Academy Press.

14. S. Philipp. 1999. Race and gender differences in adolescent peer group approval of leisure activities. *Journal of Leisure Research* 26: 99–118.

15. Joe R. Feagin and Clairece B. Feagin. 1978. *Discrimination American Style: Institutional Racism and Sexism.* Englewood Cliffs, NJ: Prentice-Hall, 19–42.

INDEX

203